Editing: Stefan J. Malecek, Ph. D. and Diana Bonnici

THE DOJO

THE ANCIENT WISDOM OF INTEGRATIVE
LEADERSHIP FOR THE MODERN ENTREPRENEUR

TONY BONNICI

DEDICATION

To my dear wife Amber, my life partner and best friend from the moment I laid eyes on her. She is my guiding light, always giving her unconditional love and support to me in all areas of my life. Thank you.

To Sage:
I love you and admire you. Your dedication, focus and creativity in getting what you want has been a model for me in writing this book.

To Bodhi:
I admire the way that you always hold a bright light. When I look at you, I feel the infinite possibilities in myself.

This work is lovingly dedicated to my dear wife Amber, my two boys Sage and Bodhi, and my brother Eric who is a visionary inspiration.

FORWARD

by
Renée Tillotson
Still & Moving Center

How does a person handle their child being at the threshold between life and death?

A sign of health is that we don't become undone by fear and trembling, but we take it as a message that it's time to stop struggling and look directly at what's threatening us.

Pema Chödrön

Allow me to tell you, if I may, about how Tony Bonnici handled it, together with his wife Amber, both life coaches, needing to walk their talk when it really mattered.

So many folks lose it in clutch situations. We struggle to accept what has happened. We grip with all our might onto a reality that no longer IS. We basically check out of the present moment by blaming the universe, spinning off into would have, could have, should have.

How willing and prepared to stay fully present in the moment is a person, a parent in this case? How could WE best face an overwhelming situation? What if we took a deep, huge lungful of air and chose to Be Here Now, no matter what, no matter how awful, no matter how scary? What if we looked the situation in the eyeball and stared it down?

I asked Tony and Amber what techniques or principles they relied upon to get through their family's near-brush with mortality. Here's their story.

Their sixteen-year-old son Sage has been learning to free dive in the ocean - we're talking depths of 100 feet with no breathing equipment. A few weekends ago he made some of those very deep dives despite some head congestion. On that Monday he was unable to "clear" his ears, so he resurfaced after diving only 45 feet. On Tuesday morning he awoke with a significant earache. By Wednesday, he had a fever brewing and something dripping out of his ears, so Amber made a doctor's appointment.

On Thursday morning Sage went into body shakes. Amber loaded him into the car and headed straight for the closest hospital in Kona. On their way, Sage went into a seizure for the first time in his life – eyes rolled back in his head, motionless and completely unresponsive. Can you imagine having to keep driving to reach the hospital while your kid is in seizure?!? Amber called upon Jesus, ancestors and angels to help her through it.

She kept the presence of mind to call 911 while driving, which directed her to a nearby fire station, where Sage was stabilized and taken to the hospital by ambulance.

Tony took Amber's place at the hospital Thursday afternoon so that Amber could go home to their younger son Bodhi. After Amber left, Sage suddenly made a huge turn for the worse. His temperature soared and within a matter of minutes he again went into a full seizure.

As Tony describes that event in the Kona hospital, it took all his life's training and practice to watch his son writhing on the hospital bed as the room filled with more and more medical personnel. To stay grounded, Tony took in every detail, counting the number of doctors and nurses, noting the job that each of them was doing to keep Sage alive, as his vital signs dropped.

Tony tells me about the practice he learned from his dad, a Zen Roshi, of consciously allowing his emotions and feelings to well up, the sensation filling him to just the chin level – very much like a person managing to keep their chin above water so that they don't sink and drown. As he surveyed the hospital room, Tony quivered with the felt sense of the moment's magnitude.

Then Tony saw a staff member come into the room with the "paddles" used to shock a patient's heart back into activity after a cardiac arrest. He realized for the first time how close they were to losing his son.

At that point, Tony recalls using a different technique to stay present. Instead of feeling all the emotions with which his body was reacting to the situation, he threw up a wall, a shield. Tony had learned this method for deflecting energy – in this case, the energy of emotion – from his decades of judo training. There was no spare consciousness available for his feelings. He now needed to give full attention to willing Sage into life, willing him to hold on, to stay with them.

Sage regained consciousness, and they did not use the "paddles" on him, yet one of the doctors told Tony to call Amber and have her come to the hospital immediately. I can just imagine how terrifying that directive must have been – to call his wife in to possibly say goodbye to their first child. I get shaky just thinking/ feeling about it. But the two of them held it together, Amber quickly dropping their younger son off with a willing neighbor.

The medical team did a spinal tap on Sage, looking for bacteria in the spinal fluid, then Amber got into the plane that medevacked Sage from the island of Hawaii to the Kapiolani Medical Center for Women and Children on our island of O'ahu. Sage needed more specialized care than Kona could provide.

Amber went into Mother Bear modality, caring for and protecting her cub. This is a form of the warrior mode that Amber teaches in her Women Unleashed retreats. For seven nights and days, Amber barely left Sage's bedside. She "slept" on a tiny flat cot beside him, awaking at least every two hours when the nurses came in or when Sage came down with ferocious headaches. His ears were still dripping a substance out of them, and he was on double antibiotics, intravenously, for three hours at a stretch, three times a day, with pain meds every 3 hours for his head.

Tony had immediately followed his son and wife to O'ahu and was staying at our house. He and Amber texted throughout the nights to stay on top of Sage's situation. During this phase, to keep fear from overwhelming him, Tony reports that he had to stay "curious". Instead of passively allowing his scared thoughts to run rampant, he and Amber would actively, respectfully question the doctors on the symptoms, the possible causes, and all their potential treatments for Sage's condition. Using his mind in this way kept Tony present.

Amber's two requests from the hospital were for an artist's drawing pad and a yoga mat. As a painter, she relied on her art and her writing to journal her mental and emotional way through the experience, keeping her body fresh with yoga.

She tracked all her emotions – such as guilt at having taken 2 minutes to get off her zoom call with several hundred clients, to respond to Sage back home when he first started feeling body shakes coming on. She allowed herself to really FEEL those emotions, and then let them go.

During all that time, Tony and Amber endured the agony of NOT KNOWING what was wrong with their boy. With an excellent team of doctors, from an infectious disease specialist, a neurosurgeon, an eye specialist, to ear-nose and throat doctors, no one could definitively diagnose him. These parents stayed in the unknowing without spinning out. Throughout their ordeal, while talking with me, they were each able to ask me about my life and what was going on with me, and truly listen, there in the moment, then move back to attending Sage. Admirable presence.

Another method of staying grounded – when part of themselves wanted to retreat into fear – was to call upon their support network. Amber and Tony never allowed themselves to get into a situation of feeling all alone. They remembered what they teach: that we are all part of an interconnected fabric of family, friends and others who want to help. They put out the word that they needed everyone's prayers, blessings, and meditations to get through this nightmare. The response was immediate and overwhelming. Hundreds of emails, texts, cards, and flowers flooded in, with meals sent to the hospital, neighbors watching the dog and house, and grandparents caring for their younger son. They knew they were not alone!

After a week, the doctors felt it safe to move Sage out of ICU and into a regular hospital room, even though they still did not know exactly what they were treating. Amber relinquished her place at Sage's bedside to get a couple nights of real sleep at our house, then flew home to their son Bodhi. Tony now moved into the hospital as Sage's full-time advocate and gatekeeper.

For any of us who have spent time in a hospital, which is supposed to be a place of rest for recuperation, we know that it's really not that quiet or peaceful a place. Tony stayed present by taking it on as his duty to teach ninja techniques to every individual who entered Sage's room, teaching them to assess the situation (like, is the kid sleeping while I'm shoving the door open, calling out "Dinner"?), then adjust their volume accordingly, and communicate appropriately. At one point he had to give a politely intense lecture to a group of 5 doctors who unceremoniously barged into the room, talking loudly and mostly about Sage as if he couldn't hear or understand them.

From his years of training in the Mankind Project, Tony stayed in the moment by self-monitoring while he was protecting and advocating for Sage. We've all met obnoxious, overprotective parents. That wasn't Tony. He kept his intensity blunted instead of blaring, showing his gratitude for all the excellent care they were receiving – mixed in with a few encounters with staff who just didn't get it. In a steady, self-restrained way, Tony just made sure Sage got the care he needed.

I'm happy to tell you that two weeks after Sage was admitted to Kapiolani, the doctors released him with a diagnosis of meningitis, from which he was well on his way to recovery. His eardrum had burst, on both the outside and the inside to the brain. Can you imagine?

Tony, Amber, and Bodhi were all at the hospital to fly home with him.

And that's how SOME people – some very mature people who have trained themselves to truly stay present in the moment – handled their kid almost dying. Amazing, yeah?

> May we continue to open our hearts and minds,
> In order to work ceaselessly for the benefit of all beings.
> May we go to the places that scare us.
> May we lead the life of a warrior.

PEMA CHÖDRÖN

PREFACE

I was living in Hawaii. I had three companies in California and two companies in Hawaii. I was so focused on my businesses that I wasn't there for my wife, Amber and my sons, Bodhi and Sage. I was feeling empty, lost and missing what was most important to my life. I knew I had to live my life differently so I could focus on what was really important to me as an entrepreneur, father, husband, and man!

In Part One of this book, I share my life journey and the lessons I've experienced. I share the values and beliefs I learned as a child and young adult and how I lost focus on these values. As I started working, I became so focused on work and on producing money that I forgot the rest of my life. I had several dramatic wake-up calls that allowed me to understand what my priorities were. Through these experiences, I developed a methodology that has helped me and my clients live a fulling life- about more than just making money.

In Part Two, I share my methodology for becoming an Integrated Leader. You'll learn to live a fulfilling, joyful, productive life by daily integrating the four areas of your life of work/legacy, physical, relationships, and spiritual. Exploring these four quadrants within a structure of the Dojo, which is a place of brutal honesty and practice, allows you to live your fullest dream and ideals of life in an integrated way. The experiences in one quadrant affects all the others. We explore these quadrants through the Monk—looking at your Core beliefs and limiting thoughts; the Sage—creating a Dream Vision for each quadrant; the Samurai—deeply listening and creating an action plan to create the Vision; and the Sensei—implementing these in your daily life and leaving a legacy in the world. Living as an Integrated

Leader. As an Integrated Leader you live your life in integrity with your goals and visions in all areas of your life; and you teach, promote and encourage others to live from their most authentic and highest vision.

In Parts Three and Four, I share the Journey some of my clients have taken and the lessons they have implemented to live as an Integrated Leader as well as lessons for you to integrate into your life now.

In Part Five I invite you to join me to explore your life and live as an Integrated Leader so that you feel fulfilled and experience your dream in all areas of your life.

In this book, I give concrete exercises and questions that help you discover how you want to live your life. I walk closely with my clients, holding the vision and providing guidance so that you can live as an Integrated Leader in all areas of your life.

May this book inspire you to live and create the life that you have always dreamed, and do so from a place of excitement, love, and ease. Allow your body/mind/soul to dream bigger than you have ever thought possible.

This kind of discipline and concentration paid dividends in all the other areas in my life.

**Jason Seaward,
CEO and Founder of Motion Recruitment**

I experience myself in a totally new way, reembodying my skills as an Integrated Leader.

**Michael Bonahan,
CEO of Wisdom Windfall,
Former Director of Boys to Men, Hawaii**

Tony has encouraged me to not only focus on growing my business and legacy but to not lose sight of my relationships, spiritual practice, and self-care.

**Renée Tillotson,
Founder of The Still & Moving Center and
The Mindful Movement Academy**

TRANSFORMING TONY

Part One

PART ONE
CHAPTER ONE

Growing Up Zen

"Click! Click!"
It was the clacking sound that my father made with his tongue every morning at 5:55 AM to begin the day. I jumped out of bed and threw on my sweats and placed my bare feet on the cold hardwood floor. I approached him with great reverence and we bowed to each other. I followed him in an intentional state as we made our way to the Shōrō (the redwood structure where the large bell and three-foot redwood striker were housed). The bell hung from a giant beam in the rafters. The entire building was made of redwood. Each strike was precise, toning eight times in the morning and again at sunset to honor the closing of the day.

My brother and I took turns every other week ringing the steel temple bell. We gathered every day, rain or shine, for this ceremonial greeting of the day. I was eight years old when we first started this practice. My walking, bowing, my every step, was purposely taken and precise. My father always made his own clothing and I will always associate the scent of fresh cotton with him. Candle light illuminated the entire interior and the air was cold, plumes of breath visible in the winter. Temple incense burned aromatically. A photograph of Suzuki Roshi, one of the lineage holders of Soto Zen Buddhism, hung prominently in the hallway of the temple where we met to begin the ceremony. From the instant I entered, I was surrounded by the living presence of sacred space.

It never struck me as odd, that just beyond the fifty-foot pine tree in my front yard, stood Jotoku-Ji (Quiet Virtue Temple). It was the temple and the home where I grew up, surrounded by oaks, redwoods and madrones, in a subdivision in Rohnert Park, up Highway 101, just fifty miles north of San Francisco in Sonoma County. The air was almost always fresh and rich, filled with the not-too-distant ocean breezes and that of thousands of trees all around us—although it could get very hot and dry in the parched summer months and bone-chilling cold in the winter.

My father had long been dedicated to the path of Buddhism and continuing the lineage of Soto Zen through teaching, writing and embodying it in his life. Soto Zen emphasizes Zazen Only, just breathing into the still center-point of gravity just two inches below the navel where you experience a deep tranquility, peace, and groundedness that guides you through everyday life and relationships.

While most fathers left the house every day to go to work, my father chose to stay home with his wife and two boys, creating a temple where he would practice and teach. When asked why he didn't go out and get a regular job, he would always respond: "Your mother and I are going to grow up with you." Our house became a thriving day care center by day for twelve children. My parents were the founders and creators of Jotoku-Ji (our home temple) that held the core teachings of Zen day and night.

My father had done his initial training in the Sonoma Mountain hills at a temple called Genjoji. I had played there extensively from age four to fourteen. I had been known to break dance in the main Zendo with the Abbot's son. Forty years later I sat in a week-long silent meditation retreat.

My father didn't live or teach Buddhism to me intellectually. His method was to be a living example of his beliefs and faith in his Core Self which is our inborn wisdom and compassion in his everyday life. He taught us to trust, to listen to our intuition, to practice daily and train at developing the sacred relationship between Core Self and thinking mind.

We would have a ceremonial meal around the altar once a month. We often chanted the Heart Sutra together as a family. He taught me to listen to the trees themselves when bonsaiing them. These were examples of my embedded training and the beauty and scope of my father's teachings.

My father was always there for us as we were growing up, always ready to assist and uplift us, to inform and guide us. One thing that he continually said to my brother and I was, "When you grow up and move out, I'll go on with what I need to do."

Through making that a priority when I was younger, he modeled for me the importance of the relationship between father and son. We became more connected every single day. He was and is my best friend. I continue to emulate his tradition. He is the living role model for me and my relationship with my two sons.

He kept his word to us. After we had become established on our own individual paths in the world, he went on to being more of a presence in the world, taking his lineage to a more global level.

Although it was not diagnosed until many years later, I was dyslexic and ADD. It was challenging for me to read and write, confusing the shapes and order of letters. The base of my understanding was always somatic. I absorbed many of the classic text as interpreted and taught by my father. I learned very early to trust my intuition and listen to the inner silence.

I was held back in third grade, despite my obvious intelligence, because I had difficulty reading and did not do well on tests. Even though my parents tried to get help with tutors and testing, nobody really understood ADD and dyslexia at that time. (It was not until my senior year in high school that I had the opportunity to do three weeks of tests at UC San Francisco that resulted in a definitive diagnosis.)

PART ONE
CHAPTER TWO

My Mother is an Undercover Agent

My mother has always been my agent of love and connection, bringing me the fruit of her love and labors. She guided me and validated me for doing the right things. She empowered me to not buy into or take on the judgments of other people, especially those about my dyslexia or my difficulty reading and writing. I call her "undercover agent" because she never talks about her many abilities and achievements. She always lets her actions speak for her.

She has always demonstrated a "beginner's heart/mind." She has always been very humble about her healing, metaphysics, and multi-dimensional living. She has always demonstrated an amazing ability to sort through the vast number of materials and discriminate as she shifted from Christian to Catholic to Buddhist—eventually evolving and awakening to her calling as a Buddhist priest. She lived her spiritual practice through her ability to listen and connect with other people and speak from her heart. She was always a living example of generosity and compassion.

I remember after a judo tournament in Reno where I was pretty badly injured (right ankle). I woke up the next morning with my mother's right-hand hovering three to four inches above my ankle, sending it white light with no touch. I grew up always believing that that was how healing was done. (I did not find out until I was 24 when I took my first Reiki class that was Reiki and she was a Reiki Master.)

She learned and taught about a variety of different modalities and celebrated them all with us—including celebrating Buddhas Enlightenment, Christmas, and Hanukkah with twelve day-care kids in the meditation hall where we did Buddhist ceremony every night.

My mom has always been the complete embodiment of pure love, grace and compassion. She always created adventures for my brother and me, so that we would always have great memories and fun—long hikes in the wilderness, baking bread, camping by the ocean, fresh and salt-water fishing.

After my brother and I had left the house, she returned to school, got her Master's degree and then got her Marriage and Family Counseling Certificate (MFCC) after the age of forty and has been in full-time practice ever since. She never advertises and yet she has a very full life coaching practice. All of her referrals have always been word-of-mouth. She has also been going to Cross-Fit for over seven years. She is a model of healthy self-care and fitness.

PART ONE
CHAPTER THREE

Into the Dojo and Out

At six years old, I started training in the art of judo. I was initially fearful of going into the unknown but it seemed that I had a natural ability. I was a kinesthetic kid. I was a born athlete. Physical movement and competition felt completely natural. I went to Florida, Las Vegas and Hawaii for national competitions.

When I got invited to the Junior Olympics, it was really wonderful to experience what it was like to have support from coaches and mentors at that level. I was constantly encouraged to take my performance to levels I had never before imagined. I performed extremely well for my coaches. With the intense attention to my training, going to the gym, practice and being on the mat, I lost my focus on spiritual practice. Even with my long history of growing up in a Zen Temple, training for this event took precedence—my relationships fell away too. I shut down my emotions almost totally and lost part of myself in this fierce focus.

There were many benefits. As my skill and confidence rose, I felt increasingly powerful, even invincible. I walked differently.

I talked differently. One might have even said I was arrogant, acting out my teenaged angst. I did not feel close with anyone. I pushed people away. I had no time for emotional nonsense, no time to let anyone else in. They were a burden to me. I had time only for what benefitted me. Another big gain for me was that my new attitude allowed me to hide from my shame about my dyslexia and ADD.

I was always very forward-focused—being a chameleon, being a ninja. I was constantly manipulating to get the outcomes I aimed for. I always aimed to have the "right" answer so I didn't look stupid. I didn't want other people to know that I didn't know. That way, the teachers couldn't shame me and the other students couldn't bully me. This was an early example of my unconscious motivation to avoid obstacles and resistance.

PART ONE
CHAPTER FOUR

The Entrepreneurial Adventure

I started my first business when I was eighteen. I applied the same lessons of Judo to entrepreneurship. In great detail, I visualized owning, building, and customizing exotic cars. I visualized the high-end auto shop I wanted much the same as I visualized winning the judo match before I stepped onto the mat. I had no idea how I would get there, but I could see it and feel it in my body. I always trusted that. Over the next ten years of trial and error, of many successes and failures, I made a great deal of money and I lost a fair amount too. As in any business venture, I made mistakes and so did my employees, but I kept moving forward. I always held the vision and focused on my motivation: "I'm an entrepreneur. For me, it's all about making money. That's why I am seen as successful."

Another key lesson was to vigilantly trust in my inner listening and my intuition. I knew I could create any business that I was excited about. But my working long hours and being away from my family for extended periods of time took an enormous toll on all my relationships. I was not concerned about deep connections. It would be many years until my wife and children powerfully brought that lesson home to me. It was one of the major losses I would have to suffer before I woke up to what was really most important to me.

My bank accounts were steadily filling, yet I had no spiritual practice and my most intimate relations were fading. I was all about making money. After about ten years of this deep focus on work, I realized I had to do something different. I was constantly praised by almost everyone around me because of my financial success and the image of what I thought an entrepreneur should be, but I was bored. I had a dirty little secret—I wasn't even trying any more at work. To myself, I used the label "retired." The truth was that I just didn't care any longer, though no one could see that I was hiding. It was, in many ways, similar to being an elite athlete. It came easily, but I just wasn't excited or fulfilled any longer.

My response to this lapsed interest and desire was to hire a performance coach. I dove into his guidance and got really intoxicated, higher than I had ever been on any drug. He was all about the numbers and that totally seduced me. I started working even longer hours.

I came upon the idea of "ten times-ing business." I decided I wanted to grow my business to ten times its present size. I opened four other businesses, two in Hawaii, and three more in California. I was living the dream: big house on the water; beautiful boat, all the toys.

Then I got married, and had my first child.

That first three years of Sage's life, I wasn't a dad. My wife didn't have a husband. The two of them paid the highest for my absence and focus on business. I was still operating from the place of scarcity, and made up the story that Amber would leave if I didn't bring in a certain amount of money every month.

PART ONE
CHAPTER FIVE

Wake Up Calls

Growing up dyslexic, I learned quickly to shut down my emotions and avoid my shame in order to function in the midst of being bullied at school or on the mat competing in Judo. I believed that other people just did not care.

BOOM! Fast forward 20 years! Looking back from this perspective, I realize how totally shut down I was emotionally. I feel great sadness about these losses. I cry as I write these words.

MY FIRST WAKE-UP CALL

2007 was our best year in business. The auto spa had ten employees, and six thousand square feet of working space. We were upgrading and customizing fifty to sixty high-end cars a month.

My wife and I bought a second home in Hawaii and I started living there full-time, flying back and forth every three weeks. I truly felt I was living the dream. Two businesses in Hawaii and three in California! Then, 2008 brought the massive financial crash. My business almost overnight went from eighty percent cash and twenty percent accounts receivable to ninety percent accounts receivable. No one was spending cash.

An incident occurred when one of my business partners and I were flying to Las Vegas for a trade show. We were waiting to board the plane at the airport when my phone rang. My bookkeeper tearfully told me we were $30,000 short for payroll. I felt like I was going to explode. I was freaking out on the inside, heart racing, palms sweating. On the outside, I looked calm, cool and collected. I was dressed to impress in slacks and a sport coat. I was looking good. I was exerting every effort to hold it all together. As I stood next to my business partner, I felt completely alone. I threw cold water on my face in the bathroom and looked in the mirror. I did not want not to be alive. I walked out of the bathroom and looked my partner in the eyes. Then I laid it all out, told him the complete truth about everything. He looked at me for a few seconds that felt like forever. "We got this," he said, and started throwing out ideas that were the exact opposite of my own. Then he came up with a suggestion that scared me the most. "Call your wife."

She was in Oregon completing a workshop. "Oh, hell no!" I said to myself.

I had to take a few moments to calm down before I dialed her number. "Hey baby," she said to me. I felt the calming presence in her voice flood through me, but I couldn't talk. I started crying and could not stop. Then she said, "Tell me what's happening!"

I felt like the cork that had been popped out of a champagne bottle. I had spent ten years believing I was keeping it all together and it came to an end there at the airport. There were hundreds of people all around me and I just didn't care. I had been cracked open and could not stop.

Amber just listened, and let me go on until I stopped. When they announced that it was time to board the plane, all I could say was "Fuck! No money. I'm done." Amber simply said, "Thank you for telling me the truth. We'll transfer the money to cover payroll. Just get on the plane and we'll talk when you get here." I started crying again, just totally lost it as I was boarding the plane. I had never felt such incredible support before in my life. Thank you, Carlos and Amber. I love you. By the time we landed in Las Vegas, Amber had transferred the money from savings to cover payroll while my partner and I went to the trade show.

The fact that I had been spending enormous amounts of time away from my kids and my partner, coupled with the loss of savings, led to the inevitable conclusion to close all three of my businesses in California, two of which I had been growing for 20 years. This started my journey for teaching and coaching. This was the push I needed to open myself to open to expanding in a new direction.

LIFE LESSONS

1. You don't lose power by being vulnerable and transparent- it encourages people to come closer to you.

2. Trust your gut. Your ego will always try to stop you.

3. Be willing to open up to feel your feelings and share them.

MY SECOND WAKE UP CALL

The date was February 7, 2008. I'll never forget. 5:00 AM Thursday (and Friday is payday) when my bookkeeper called to tell me again that we were $50,000 short of making payroll and expenses for the month. I do not believe I even flinched as I shut down emotionally and hid the fear, rage and anger that raced through my body. I did my best to ignore what I was feeling. I acted like all was well. I had experienced all of this before. I simply ignored it and moved on.

I got this!

Ten minutes later, Amber went into labor. I came up with what I thought was a great plan—focus on the business, create the money before she transitions, and don't feel anything. Again, I felt as if my insides were going to explode while on the outside, I maintained a cool façade. Oh, by the way, did I mention that my office was right next door to the master bedroom and we were having a home birth, a water birth in our own bedroom?

I got Amber set up and then I went back to work. Focus. Focus. Focus. "Be right there, honey." I would check on Amber between making calls to collect money as I listened to her doing her chanting in the other room.

"I'm having a baby and I'm worried about work? WTF?"

"Keep it together," I would say over and over to myself.
The contractions kept getting closer and closer together. I

had made about fifty calls by the time her contractions got so close that I couldn't talk on the phone anymore. I had actually managed to create enough income to pay the bills and payroll.

I did it! I did it! I'm having a baby!

When I "woke up," as if from a very strange dream, I was in the tub, completely drenched head-to-toe, as Amber bore down giving her final push for our new baby to come into this world. It felt like everything was moving in slow motion, as if I could almost count the frames of my life flickering by.

Suddenly, everything was feeling! I could feel everything! I was wet. I was scared. I was happy, sad, even angry all at the same time. When she pushed and roared, I felt the crown of my little one's head. I looked at him, brought him up from the water and over to my dear Amber's chest. I was so filled with love. I was crying uncontrollably. I was surrounded and filled with love. Nothing but love.

All I could do was look at my new son Bodhi, Sage and my beautiful wife Amber. There was nothing else in the Universe but my family filled with Love and Joy.

In the Buddhist tradition, death, old age, sickness and health are guaranteed to bring you back fully into your body. Experiencing childbirth did that for me. I had spent thirty years trying not to feel. Now everything, simply everything, was feelings. I too had been born anew that day, filled with a love and joy I had not known for a very long time.

My mind kept wanting to make some kind of cognitive sense of all that had just happened, asking questions and wanting me to focus on mental information.

The only way I could find to express this in my body was to say, "Let's do this again," at which point Amber gave me the Look of Death! I don't recommend saying that right after delivery.

Great! Now what?

My son Bodhi, is now fourteen years old. We share a metaphorical birthday. That day my journey through Life started again. I woke up to the wonderful experience of feeling emotions in my body.

LIFE LESSONS

1.   Permission to live your life in a different way.

2.   You can be a leader and feel at the same time. It's all just energy in your body.

3.   You don't have to hide your emotions. You get to feel them, safely express them and move on.

4.   Feel everything: Mad, Sad, Happy, Fear, Shame, Peaceful, Powerful, Self-Loving and everything in between.

5.   Your feelings are energetic messages from your body. If you stop allowing even one feeling, all of your feelings will suffer.

6.   Your mind is very powerful. Even after fourteen years of training and practicing transparency, I can still feel my nagging mental resistance while writing this.

7.   There is another way to do business and daily living to stay connected to your family, your life, and spirituality... get ready to enter The Dojo.

THE METHOD

Part Two

PART TWO
CHAPTER SIX

The Dojo

In this section we explore my methodology to help you live as an Integrated Leader. In my Business Coaching practice, I teach you to live a fulfilling, joyful, productive life by daily integrating the four areas of your life of work/legacy, physical, relationships and spiritual. We explore living as an Integrated Leader by using the Monk, Sage, Samurai and Sensei pillars within the container of the Dojo. As an Integrated Leader you live your life in integrity with your goals and visions; and you teach, promote and encourage others to live from their most authentic and highest vision.

I have developed the ideas for my methodology utilizing the image of the Dojo. Dojo literally translates from the Japanese as "Buddhist seminary drill hall," though it is translated from the Sanskrit as the "seat of wisdom." The Dojo is a place of brutal honesty and practice. I have chosen this powerful word as a metaphor for my personal work. I have identified myself with and immersed myself in the Dojo, awakening and integrating my life. It is therefore both grounding and inspiring for continuing progress.

It is the actual working environment in which intense focus, compassion, hard work and accomplishment meet. It is, in my estimation, the ideal environment for both discipline and maximum personal growth.

This is the place of practice where you step onto the mat and you take a hard look at how you are showing up in all areas of your life. This is where you leave your ego at the door and lean into those edges of your life like you have never done before. The dojo is where you have my support right next to you, shoulder-to-shoulder, helping you delve deeply into your truth, and challenging you in ways you never thought possible.

THE FOUR PILLARS

The four pillars of the Dojo hold space by defining your interior purpose and expanding your opportunities for work/legacy, physical, relationships, and spiritual life in all of the ways that you find most meaningful, uplifting and productive. These four pillars will be used constantly to explain and expand the vision and actions of the Integrated Leader in order to live your vision of wholeness and growth. The four pillars are: Monk; Sage; Samurai; and Sensei.

MONK

The Monk focuses on integrating your life and understanding your core feelings, beliefs and thinking. It is from these core feelings, beliefs and thinking that you have created a personal reality. We explore your outdated ideas that no longer serve you and limit your ability to live as an Integrated Leader and live a well-rounded, balanced and challenging life in every aspect of your life.

SAGE

The Sage focuses on visioning. Listening to and utilizing your inner resources, intuition and inner knowledge allows you to see beyond the ordinary. We will envision new possibilities and opportunities beyond what you could have previously imagined and dream. Living in and from this vision, allows you to live a fuller, richer integrated life with more possibilities in every quadrant.

SAMURAI

The Samurai focuses on strategy. When the energy of the Monk and the Sage are integrated, working together with a clear vision driving your life, a naturally unfolding strategy occurs to critically direct your plan and actions. The way of the Samurai embraces the path by using the clarity and incisiveness of a sword. In each step forward within the intimate plan you have envision, you proceed confidently, listening deeply for directions to each new step and take action.

SENSEI

The Sensei focuses on leading by example and empowering others. In this pillar you have done the deep and demanding personal work to become clear and skilled in living as an Integrated Leader. It is in this quadrant, when reached naturally and developed fully, that the Monk, the Sage, and the Samurai are integrated into the Sensei. The Sensei becomes the center around which all of these aspects revolve. This is where you walk your talk and talk your walk—moving in and living from your vision in each quadrant simultaneously. The Sensei's life embodies all that you preach and teach in all areas of your life. The Sensei constantly encourages others to be their very best and live their highest potential.

PART TWO
CHAPTER SEVEN

The Four Quadrants

In the Dojo, using the four pillars of Monk, Sage, Samurai and Sensei we take a deeper look into the four quadrants. The four quadrants are the four areas in your life that we work with to create a balanced and integrated life. The four quadrants are work/legacy, physical, relationship and spiritual. With the four pillars we are able to explore and understand how you relate to the four quadrants in your life so that you can live your fullest life as an Integrated Leader.

In this chapter we explore on a deeper level the meaning of the way you live in the four quadrants as an Integrated Leader. We explore how to purposefully and consciously balance your life in all four of the major quadrants. The success of your business, company or organization manifests as you focus your full life in the work/legacy, physical, relationships and spiritual simultaneously. Living as an Integrated Leader is equally challenging and growth-producing in all areas. To truly be a success at anything, you learn to work and access all four quadrants. Each quadrant strengthens and enhances the other quadrants. An Integrated Leader is well-rounded, balanced, and challenged in all four quadrants.

Work/Legacy

Conscientiously leading your business with vision and direction, this area lets your business grow exponentially as you move forward in all four quadrants with awareness and balance.

Legacy is what you will be remembered by when you leave your position of responsibility. It is what you have done of service that makes a difference on the planet. Shifting attention to service in legacy will genuinely be about your desire to give, not just about money or what new worlds you might conquer. Being in a place of service, you will constantly be open to growth and new opportunities.

Physical

Regular daily bodily movement, health awareness and self-care.

Relationships

Intimacy and communication with your partner, children, family members, friends and colleagues all around the world.

Spiritual

Creating quiet time for yourself to connect with the present moment. To connect with God, Inner Wisdom. To listen to your own deepest truth.

PART TWO
CHAPTER EIGHT

Which Quadrant is your Challenge?

I thought my life was working really well because my business/work life was very full and involved. I made it up that I had what I thought was a perfect marriage and that I was deeply involved in it. "Oh, I'm really good at relationships. I love my wife. We have a deep relationship," but what I really wanted was a deeper, healthier, honest, and more meaningful and intimate relationship with my wife. I was hiding who I was and holding back.

At a speaking engagement, one of the women participants said even thinking about these four quadrants generated such fear in her belly that she shut down completely. That was a perfect example of how quickly the mind will disavow what you feel, override what your heart senses. But then she had the courage to admit that the spiritual quadrant was her most difficult arena, that it was a struggle for her to even acknowledge that it had importance to her at all.

Now, take a big breath and let's go deeper.

Each quadrant of work/legacy, physical, relationships and spiritual represents a vital force in your life, though one or more may be less energized or appealing to you. Number each of your quadrants, beginning with your favorite (or strongest) as #1, you might call it your zone of genius where you thrive and have the most fun. Then, work down through the rest of the quadrants with your weakest (or least favorite) as #4, the arena you try to most avoid or into which you put the least energy. This is the one that needs the most attention.

At this point, questions will inevitably arise, perhaps as feelings in your body or thoughts, around this area of your life. I realized that for me it was fear. I was scared to look at my relationship with my wife (my #4) with the same level of attention as I was with my business. Business was relatively easy, but diving deeper into my relationship with my wife was so much more difficult and painful—despite the fact that I loved her deeply.

Even the thought of sharing a Relationship Coach with her scared the living daylights out of me—so that is exactly what we chose to do, stepping into our greatest fear. By doing this our intimacy and our relationship were impacted in ways we could never have imagined. The net result of that deepening had a profound effect on the other areas of my life: my spiritual practice, my body and even my legacy and work life.

WRITING EXERCISE: Challenge Quadrant

Right now, jot down that one thing that is #4, the one you don't want to talk about. Acknowledge it within yourself. Give it a form. Make it visible. What one small step can you do to work on this area?

PART TWO
CHAPTER NINE

The Monk: Truth

The Monk is the first pillar where you explore your thoughts and the core beliefs that shape your life in each of the four quadrants of your life of work/legacy, physical, relationships and spiritual. What beliefs, positive and negative, do you hold onto, based on past experience, that may shape or limit your ability to move forward in your life? The Monk is about examining how you show up. The Monk is about looking honestly at how you present yourself, how you step onto the mat, and reveal your true self and hold nothing back.

The Monk is the arena where you take a look at yourself in each quadrant. This includes your thoughts as well as your emotions, and how they are expressed in your life. The arena of the Monk is about telling the utter naked truth to yourself, being totally honest about your work/legacy, physical well-being, relationships, and spiritual connection.

I walk with you and guide you and we do this work together through the lens of the Integrated Leader, challenging you in all areas. We start with looking at where you are putting your energy and where you are withholding it. If you are primarily focused on work and legacy, then your relationship, spiritual practice, or your body may be suffering. It may mean that you're not leaning into your edge, perhaps not challenging yourself in all areas. If one quadrant is out of balance, the other quadrants are affected. It is not possible to experience all of them fully if you are suppressing one of them. Now we will explore the Monk in each of the four quadrants in depth.

Work

Within this Monk pillar, we examine the work quadrant by taking a dive into your beliefs about the nature and quality of your work, and how you invest yourself in your work. Do you go to work to participate deeply and empower your associates to really be the best that they can be? Do you create mastery in your work environment? Are you impeccable in setting the foundational structure around work as you explore your values (based on your vision) for your company? Are you in synch with the existing structures? Are you seeking to create new systems? What is your orientation to team-building, meeting schedules, check-ins? How are you empowering your team to be the best that they can be, and allow your team autonomy and to excel?

Is the work you are doing and the manner in which you are accomplishing it fulfilling for you? Does your work resonate with your heart's desires? Are you expending your energies at the workplace in a healthy way? Are there areas of work that would benefit from more of your energy to help grow or expand your company? Do you harbor a belief that you have to work nonstop to be successful? Is it okay for you to truly succeed and be a success? Do you feel a connection with your customers and your ability to succeed? Do you feel related to them as fellow human beings? Are you showing up as a central influence as a business owner and visionary holding the foundation of your company? A thorough exploration of the perceived limitations in your thinking can reveal how you are limiting or stopping yourself from reaching your desired way of being, and the outcomes you wish to achieve at work. Are you open to allowing yourself to be creative and to dream of possibilities and a future you design? Are you being an open creative channel at the workplace and encouraging others to be their best? Do you communicate openly, honestly, freely?

Legacy

For legacy and mission work, we focus on a world mission, one that is embracing of global change and strategy—a mission that can and will affect many people, if not humanity as a whole. Open your mind and heart. See what you can imagine, what might be possible. This is a big give back. This is an example of living from a place of service. This is an opportunity to contribute to the world and create a legacy that will outlive you; one that will reverberate for years, if not decades, beyond your passing.

Legacy is perhaps the only thing that will have any meaning when you are gone.

You might ask why we do legacy work. In creating your vision that includes helping others, you actually shift the focus of your attention from personal gain to the greater good. In a place of giving and service, you reach out beyond your most personal concerns to potentially open to unlimited growth and opportunities far beyond what you may have been aware, exponentially opening you up to more success in all areas. In this way, giving truly is receiving.

In this aspect of this work, we explore your true beliefs of service and make critical decisions about the impact you wish to make on humanity and the planet. If you imagine a future time when you no longer exist in human form, what would be the legacy that you want to leave, not only for your children, but for the planet itself? What will be the effects would you like to be remembered in perpetuity? How will you put your love into action in such a way that it will survive you, perhaps even as a legacy to and through future generations of your family and business interests? How do you see that you might leave the world a better place than it was when you came?

Physical

In this Monk pillar, we examine your beliefs about self-care and what activities you may or may not be doing on a daily basis to take care of your physical health. What are eating and drinking? Are you sleeping well and regularly? Do you do daily self-care?

Are you getting some form of exercise to further the care of your body? Are you leaning into a personal edge where you are challenging yourself (even just slightly) every single day? Do you feel you are stepping up into greater self-care, especially in your morning rituals?

Relationships

In this Monk pillar, we question are you satisfied with the depth and quality of intimacy and connectedness in your relationships? Who has inspired you along the road of your life? Have you examined the foundation of your interactions with others, the beliefs and falsehoods you may have inherited, perhaps without examining them—including those acquired as a child? Who have you interacted with that has had an impact on you, how you are in the world and who you are? How have you been touched by the presence of loved ones and others, even strangers, through the course of your many, many acts of relating—from casual encounters to those lasting a lifetime? You have many different levels of intimacy that you have developed and held with your spouse, friends, children, work mates, employees, employers, and the countless individuals you encounter on a daily basis. How much work and awareness do you put into cultivating quality relationships in your life?

Spiritual

Within the Monk pillar, we will explore what does spirituality mean to you? This does not refer to any specific religion per se, but explores how you connect to Spirit by whatever name in whatever format you experience it. This is not an intellectual concept. It speaks to the practice you use to connect to your inner truth, that deepest sense of reverence and connection to the entire Universe, to your gut instincts, or what you consider to be your Higher Power. Have you closely examined the beliefs of your childhood religious teachings? Are they still important and real to you? It is through the practice of deep listening to yourself that you will be guided into a deeper trust and intimacy, letting you know when your resistance to change may be directing you in other than the healthiest of directions. Many times, this resistance is due to old and outmoded beliefs systems that need examination. Do you have a regular spiritual practice? Do you make time on a daily basis to connect with and cultivate that place inside of you that gives you the opportunity to listen to that God, your Inner Wisdom, the Great Mother?

WRITING EXERCISE: Your Eulogy

I have an exercise I use with my clients to help them connect with their legacy. Write up your own eulogy as if it is being written for your actual final service. Address what you want to be included, not only in the writing but in the emotions and memories that will be mentioned in memorializing your passing. More specifically what difference might you have made on this planet. What impact have you made on the lives of others?

PART TWO
CHAPTER TEN

The Monk: Integrating the Person

Scientists now say that the body has two brains—the familiar one in the skull and the lesser-known but vitally important one found in human gut.

**Science in Hawai'i Na Hana Ma Ka Ahupun'a:
A Culturally Sensitive Curriculum Project**

We cannot selectively numb emotions. When we numb the painful emotions, we also numb the positive emotions.

Brené Brown

THREE AREAS OF THE BODY

Working with The Monk, we focus on three areas in your body. You can be aware and operate from each of these areas. The object is to recognize and be in relationship with all three simultaneously and separately.

1. Thinking 2. Feeling 3. Gut or Core instinct

Thinking

Thinking has always been the most important aspect of being an entrepreneur, using thinking to map out the path through the day and to create, manifest, design and plan. Thinking underlines our strategy for surviving in the world, figuring things out and being able to talk about the discoveries and revelations throughout our lives. This is a very important area that we deeply explore through our limiting beliefs, our core thoughts, our vision, our plan and implementing our action.

Feeling

In the earliest days of being an entrepreneur, I sincerely thought that feelings were voodoo in business. I did not find them acceptable and kept myself apart from them while working. I was able to trust my gut, trust my thinking and not feel a thing. Have you ever experienced that as an entrepreneur?

In this work you will discover that being able to actually feel what's alive in your body and your emotions is a powerful ally for learning to trust yourself and express who you are, being entirely yourself as an entrepreneur in the world and changing your life in all four quadrants.

FIVE BASIC EMOTIONS

There are many emotions, but the five core essential ones are: mad, sad, glad, fear and shame.

Take a deep breath. What do you feel, and where do you feel it in your body when I mention emotions? What do you feel NOW? Many people are frequently not aware of their emotions. They are hidden under obscuring clouds of old thoughts and memories. Maybe there are some which you are not in touch with yet. What would that feeling be: mad, sad, glad, fear, or shame?"

The key to this really wonderful and powerful arena is being able to locate where in your body you are feeling what emotion. I have discovered I feel shame in my legs, anger in my belly or fear in my chest. Once I learn where my feelings are actually expressing themselves in my body, I can begin to trust my body more. Then I can begin to trust and operate on what my body is telling me. If I am clear about what I am feeling, I don't get confused. If I am aware that I am feeling fear in my chest area, I will immediately understand that it is not shame or anger. If I can connect the feeling and my body I can make appropriate decisions and actions.

Sometimes my mind will confuse what I am feeling and give it a voice. Being completely honest with my wife, children and all relationships and communicating my true and real feelings to them—whatever the circumstances, including my appropriate anger has been extremely transforming because I am no longer afraid to identify and express my emotions.

By attempting to shut down or suppress my "bad" emotions, I ended up suppressing all of my emotions to some extent. If, for example, you are feeling joy in your life (and suppressing anger on whatever level), what you are feeling may be contaminated by what you are not expressing. You will not be touching joy, which is full, open and unrestrained. Anger is healthy if it is expressed properly, and shared in safe and healthy ways. It is only when anger is suppressed that it builds strength and power; and then it may become dangerous and even violent.

For many people, being glad is the hardest emotion to feel and express. It requires that you feel vulnerable when you open to experiencing glad or happiness to embrace deep joy and love. Through Monk we explore what emotions are challenging you and how to better express them in each of the four quadrants.

Gut Instinct

In Hawaiian we say "Na'au" for gut instinct. It is also called Listening to God, Inner Wisdom and Knowing, Core Self, Hara, or Tandem. By developing a relationship with our Inner Knowing, we experience a deeper relationship with our true Inner Self below our ego thoughts. As we practice connecting to this Inner Wisdom, we actually trust it more deeply and readily and apply it more often in our life.

There are many valid and wonderful practices to connect with this Inner Wisdom. When I coach, we practice this listening through Zazen meditation. In this form of meditation, we breathe deeply into our lower abdomen and are aware of our breath. As we breathe, thoughts will come. The mind is meant to think. But Suzuki Roshi would say "Open the front door and the back door and let your thoughts come and go. Do not invite them for tea." When a thought comes and we get caught, we return to our breath. This way we learn to not attach to our thoughts that drive us but to come from a place beneath the ego protection, live in the present moment, and move forward toward our vision.

The greatest gifts my mother ever gave me were to trust my inner promptings, to listen to what my gut tells me, and to override the inhibitions of my thoughts so I don't ignore this higher order of intelligence and knowledge. The brain learns to stay in its comfort zone (driven by old and antiquated experiences) and to maintain the status quo. Old core beliefs may tell you "It's not safe," or "You are unworthy of success" or any of a number of "good" reasons that will stop you from moving forward, trusting yourself, your vision and your goals. It does not mean we don't listen to the warnings, but we can choose whether they are valid or not and if we want to act on them.

The more you experience the wonderful power and beauty of your Inner Listening, the less resistance you will have. It's very powerful to feel your gut instinct and watch your brain attempt to suppress it. As you learn to trust your gut, the more your Truth and Inner Wisdom will guide you.

Live in your Na'au. Start listening and having a relationship with your gut. It is the beginning of knowing and the acknowledgement of your actual needs and how to manifest them in your life.

PART TWO
CHAPTER ELEVEN

Jason and The Monk

Jason had been an entrepreneur for 20 years, living in New Zealand. His company was doing over $2 million a year in revenue and growing very fast when we met. Jason had been actively pursuing the growth of his business interests, daily expanding on a regular basis; but he had no foundation for healthy growth with conscious strategies of how to balance this rapid growth. He expressed that he was almost feeling out of control. He was, in effect, out of touch with himself. As the company grew, the more complex problems became.

Jason's intention was to find greater support to build a stronger foundation for himself and the growth of his company. He also wanted to improve his very limited personal life. He wanted to develop his ability to take on that level of higher responsibility both with his business and his personal life, integrating all the areas of his life as an Integrated Leader.

As we entered the Dojo, we began looking at all the quadrants from the perspective of the Monk. Together we explored how he had been limiting himself with his belief systems, and how he could use this work to challenge himself in ways he had previously believed impossible.

Work/Legacy

Jason believed he needed to be closed off emotionally in order to excel as a boss and hit the numbers he had insisted upon. He feared his vulnerability and transparency. He saw them as weakness. When he showed up at the workplace, he did not do so as a Leader, as a man of power and being a mentor, nurturing the next generation of leaders for his company. He was not showing up as a visionary business owner who was holding the foundation for the company with a vision and structures. Therefore, he tended to hire employees who were needy and required a great deal of high maintenance and attention. He did not have the structures and guidelines in place to handle his expansion and to be clear on his employees' responsibilities.

He had never formulated a personal mission to make an impact on the planet. He did not believe he could impact the world, that it was safer for him was to "stay small" because he felt that he had "worked too hard already. I will be exhausted if I grow bigger or expand to mission work."

Physical

Jason had devoted a tremendous amount of time to this quadrant and was in great shape. Even so, he was not really challenging himself. He was playing at a 50% level being an athlete, believing he could do just enough to look good and be in shape, but he never leaned into his edge. He really did not believe he needed to challenge himself because of his fear that he could be injured and that there was no benefit to playing full out.

Relationships

In most of his relationships, Jason interacted in a very superficial manner. He truly felt he "did not have the time" to invest his energy into his family and friends. His relationships with women were equally shallow. He expressed his distaste and fear of being "in uncomfortable positions or situations." He feared sharing more than his superficial self.

Spiritual

In the Monk Pillar we looked at the absence of a daily spiritual practice in Jason's life. He sincerely believed that he "did not have time, and it doesn't have any value," leading him to declare that he did not "get up and meditate." Other things were more important. He was choosing not to connect with the place of quiet inside of himself that would give him the opportunity for greater listening and to cultivate his gut instinct, his Inner Knowing.

This deep dive into the Monk and his core beliefs helped Jason to understand how he had been holding himself back from moving deeply into all four quadrants of his life with equal love and energy. When he worked all of the quadrants with equal energy and devotion, his entire life improved. Through this essential understanding, he began to experience greater personal and interpersonal satisfaction and a much higher quality of life.

The magic happens when you explore all four quadrants with the understanding of the Monk as an Integrated Leader. Enriching one area exponentially effects all areas. The Monk pillar is a way of deepening your understanding of your life, your beliefs and will be a pillar you will explore and consistently refine throughout your life.

PART TWO
CHAPTER TWELVE

The Sage: Vision

With the awareness of integrating and understanding your core beliefs in the Monk pillar, we move into the Sage pillar. The Sage is the visionary. In the Sage pillar, we integrate all four quadrants of work/legacy, physical, relationships and spiritual into your vision. People usually think of visioning for work. But the Sage brings visioning to all four quadrants. I help you envision what you want for your life. How big a vision can you create for each quadrant? We will work with seeing it in your mind and feeling it in your body.

The Sage looks at visioning and really goes beyond what you think is possible. Being dyslexic is one of my superpowers. I don't have a box or constraint to letting my mind envision in a big way. What I can see, I create. This is what I do for my clients. I help create and hold that vision in the pillar of the Sage. We expand your vision as big as your mind wants to go, and then, we go even bigger. I fall in love with my client's dream and help them create a dream so powerful that nothing will stop them

THE SAGE

1. What is your ideal vision for your company or where you work? What is your vision for your legacy and how you impact the world?

2. What is your ideal vision for your healthiest body? What is your vision for self-care?

3. What is your ideal vision for your ultimate connection with your partner, children, family, friends and colleagues?

4. What is your ideal ultimate spiritual practice or way to connect with your gut instinct, God or your Core?

The Sage envisions and actually influences all areas of your life: work/legacy, physical, relationships and spiritual. Working on all of those areas in the same way you would work on your company or organization vision, you will exponentially grow your organization.

In the Sage Pillar, we also work with the three areas in the body:

1. Thinking Mind

2. Feeling Heart

3. Gut instinct, your Inner Knowing or Core

We work with your thinking and vision while also being aware of your feelings and your gut instinct and what is your truth. Throughout this process we notice what you are feeling—the resistances, the yes, the fear, the excitement. What are your emotions telling you about yourself and owning the vision? Listen to your gut and your deep Inner Knowing. What is your truth? What do you want to create in the world?

Now let's play. Playing with these three areas of mind, heart, and Core Wisdom is really fun because this brings you deep into the Sage and Visioning. This helps you be really creative. Dream bigger than you've ever dreamed before, where possibilities are endless. Let's go to Mars and put people on Mars. Maybe some people don't believe that yet. But, to have that kind of creative thinking and realize that they have a space ship there, and a rover on the ground over there now. Putting people on Mars is getting even closer to being a reality.

WRITING EXERCISE: 365 from Today

I'm going to invite you to close your eyes and create a vision. Write down and draw out what you want to happen 365 days from today in one quadrant. Now see in your mind's eye that vision actually happening. Feel this vision with your emotions and in your Core as if it has occurred. Experience the event taking place, where you're ringing me up and saying, "I can't believe that event that I wrote down and felt has actually happened."

That's 365 days from today. Experience the vision as it is taking place right now. Breathe as you do that. The breath is a great way to stay grounded and be present.

Now let's go out even further. Let's go three years out from today. Can you envision what would happen then? Can you let your mind, heart and Core dream a vision that far out? In three years, you will be calling me up saying, "That event that I visioned, it happened!"

Breathe into that. Slowly open your eyelids. Now write that vision down.

The Sage creates a vision of your future using your mind, heart and Core gut instinct.

The Sage envisions how you would like to see your life created, letting your imagination run wild with possibilities. Challenging your thinking into what may feel impossible. Then changing your vision to dream bigger again and again.

The vision is the place to come from, not to get to. Use the vision as your super power. Practice getting the mind and the body used to feeling the kind of energy that your vision is creating inside of you. This is the place from which you live and create.

1. Visualization—create the scene in your mind

2. Feel the sensations in the body and in your Core

3. Write it down.

4. See and feel this vision daily as if it has already occurred

5. Take one small step toward your vision.

You may resist envisioning in each your work/legacy, physical, relationship, and spiritual quadrants of your life. You may think visions are too rigid and too structured, that they stop you from trusting your Instinct. Creating your vision, and being very detailed about how that vision will look and feel, helps clarify who you want to be, and what you want to do or achieve. Then, as things get moving, you trust your Instinct and move forward while remembering what you have created as the ideal plan. Things may or may not go as you envisioned, but you continue to move the vision forward. This is where you are coming from, not just where you are wanting to go. It is necessary to have flexibility to listen so that the vision can unfold in ways you never could imagine.

You may experience your vision by creating a clear story of the outcome of the vision, as if it has already completed in as much detail as possible. This will activate or engage the body in the experience. For example, if you visualize yourself standing in your favorite location, looking around and seeing all the beauty you may get goosebumps or feel excited and joyful.

It is important to visualize and feel the vision in your body because this starts to break through your limiting beliefs or patterns that hold you back from creating that vision. The more you practice and feel the sensations in your body with that vision, the more opportunities will arise to move that vision forward. By feeling the vision daily, you show up differently in your business, in your physical and self-care, in your relationships, and in your spiritual practice.

Why

Get in touch with your Why. Why do you want this vision? What do you want to think, feel and experience? How would you be different? Your why will help you know where to come from and also encourage you as you move toward your vision.

You visualize so that you see it in your mind and feel it in your body, and show up to every part of your day, every relationship with that experience. Visualize and create that scene in your mind. Feel the sensations in the body. Trust your Inner Core sensation and information. Write it down. See and feel the vision daily. Take one small step daily from that place and fake it until you make it.

One way that I like to play with my vision is using the threshold of the doorway. When you cross a doorway to your business, you actually acknowledge that you are entering into that space as the person that has already created the kind of organization that you want. You can use a bow or a nod of the head. When you do that, you show up differently. You create differently. Your mindset is challenging your thinking. You then can do that one thing to move you forward in creating the organization you envision. Who do you have to talk to? What relationships do you have to build? How do you ultimately have to show up for your team? This can be done with your home, gym or wherever you are challenging yourself with your vision.

This is the process of the Sage Pillar and visioning. What would that look like and feel like in your body? Be the person who has actually created your vision in all four quadrants—work/legacy, physical, relationship and spiritual.

Working in the Sage pillar deeply influences how you as an individual show up for your organization, your family, your loved ones, your friends, and, of course, yourself. It is a huge gift of service on many levels. Not only does it light a fire underneath you, it is the inner vision that drives every area of your life as an Integrated Leader.

PART TWO
CHAPTER THIRTEEN

Vision and Word

One of the foundational pieces of Integrated Leadership is investigating the origin of thoughts. Most people believe in the seeming truth of their own thoughts, allowing themselves to be run by their thinking, positive and negative. And those very thoughts shape the world in which we live. Our thoughts most often arise automatically as a reaction to experiences in the present that the brain compares to situations in the past, before reacting. Negative words or communication are most often driven by previous unresolved negative experiences. On the other hand, purposeful use of generative language—speaking the future into the present, as if it already exists—generates an entirely different reality. For example, not "I will open a new business," but "I'm opening a business."

Generative versus Passive Language

There are numerous ways of seeing things and addressing your experiences. One important way is seeing your vision and speaking of it in the active (or generative) tense. When speaking in active tense, you embrace the present moment and your language embraces it. You can talk with generative language now, such as: "I teach aspiring people. I create schools. My business is growing into a million-dollar business. I have amazing relationships with my wife and children." It speaks to events as if they are already a reality. You are creating your reality. Events are not passively happening to you, or acting upon you. Using generative language keeps you focused in the present moment so that you embody the action and vitality of the moment. It is strong and positive. It literally generates or creates energy and action. Using passive language invites laziness and inaction, as if you do not create what is happening in your life. I help you work with generative language to keep your present moment always in your vision. Generative language uses language as if your vision is already actually happening. It does not say, "I will," or "I'm going to." Instead, it says, "I am in my power. I am living my Vision Now."

Generative Language in the Now

I started paying attention to the power of words and playing with using them when I was twelve years old. By then I had been suffering from the challenging effects of undiagnosed dyslexia for many years. I knew I was very intelligent, but reading and writing of any sort was extremely difficult, even painful, for me. I had learned to carefully choose what I said so I could best bluff my way through school. I had learned to hide behind a straight "B" average. I had figured out that school officials would not bother me if I did.

Long before I was legally eligible for a driver's license, I wanted to buy a truck. I started dreaming that I was going to buy my first truck. I saved my money for over three years, vowing to do so before I was sixteen. I delivered newspapers, mowed lawns, and washed dishes. I often had three jobs at the same time. Then came the grand day when I went with my mom, dad, and brother to look at vehicles at the dealership. I will never forget that day. When we got there, I saw a used truck that I knew would be mine even before I ever sat in it. I said to myself "This is it!" I remember laughing with the salesman and my parents because I didn't have a driver's license and yet I was buying a vehicle! My mom and dad had always been very supportive of my goals, dreaming with me. They were as excited as I was, having watched me through all of the years saving money for that very day. When my dad and I drove the truck home, I knew it was just the beginning of my new adventure.

I immediately saw a souped-up show truck when I looked at that 1979 Datsun pick-up long bed with its camper shell. I saw it as totally remodeled and painted with high-lacquer paint just like in the magazines. I started telling everyone, including the kids at school, "I am building a show truck." I got all kinds of responses, but only listened to the positive, supportive ones. Some of my classmates at school laughed at me and told me that it "was never going to happen." All they could see was an old farm truck. At that point, I decided not to listen to any of the people who talked down to me about my dreams and decided to just stay away from them.

I held on tightly to my vision and kept insisting that I was building my vision. Soon, a transformation started taking place. I began to have support from an auto shop teacher, and other friends joined in. We cut the top off, made the truck a convertible, shaved the door handles and customized and chromed the motor.

WRITING EXERCISE: Entrepreneurial Visioning

At one point in my coaching journey, I made a decision about who I wanted my ultimate client to be, visioning him or her into the present. I created an exercise in which I wrote out all of the details of my model client: hair color, height, weight, clothing, and personal qualities. Who is that person? What does he/she stand for? What are his/her personal characteristics, ethics and spiritual stance? I even wrote down potential names for my ideal client. I used these descriptions as a stake in the ground to establish who I wanted to work with. Using generative language, I was able to establish that having clients that understood drive and determination were important qualities for success. When I look at my current clients, they all share both of these qualities. They do the work necessary to create their vision with determination and drive. Now envision your ultimate client.

Working together you will learn to work with generative language in all four quadrants of your life. Now, it's time for you to be an Integrated Leader.

LIFE LESSONS

1. Clear and specific language is important in a Vision.

2. Words impact Reality. Speak with generative language.

3. Do not listen to negative self-talk or other's doubts.

4. Associate with people who dream big and welcome their support.

5. Embrace your vision, speak it, feel it, see it constantly in your mind as if it is already happened. This is the true power of the word.

PART TWO
CHAPTER FOURTEEN

Jason and The Sage

Jason has been both an athlete and an entrepreneur for more than thirty years. He is passionate about growing and gets the value of support. He has always been devoted to personal growth and self-development work. Let's look at his journey through the Sage pillar in all four quadrants.

Work/Legacy

In the Sage pillar, we looked at his work/legacy quadrant. Jason's company was growing at a very fast pace, but he found it difficult and challenging to determine the actual base and foundation of his business. He also did not have a vision of where he wanted his business to evolve.

So, we explored, What *could* he create? Through the Monk Pillar he understood what thinking and beliefs might interfere with his potential growth and vision. We explored how he could create an organization that defied his thinking. Jason and I started working on a vision of what he really wanted for his company. Initially his vision was to be a three-million-dollar company.

Then I asked, "What would it be like to expand the company ten times?" We discovered that the biggest company in his industry was doing about fifty-five million dollars gross a year. When I suggested that might be a figure that would challenge him, he said, "I've never even dreamed of having a company that big, but all right. Let's go there."

In the Sage pillar we explore what is it like to create and envision that. The reality begins with seeing the outcome in your mind, picturing it in as much detail as you can. Then allow yourself to feel all of the feelings that such an accomplishment might bring—the excitement, the satisfaction, the gratitude, and the joy. Listening down to your very core, and completely embracing with every cell the power and joy of having birthed an organization that is grossing fifty-five million dollars and feeling the impact that such an accomplishment might bring. Visioning that you have already accomplished it! You are seeing it as a process that's actually already happened!

Jason did not, of course, manifest this overnight. Starting with two million dollars and then, after one year growing over fifty percent, Jason decided "It's time to write up that vision and really own it on paper. I am committed—this is where I'm taking the company." He was ready to create the experience with actual visualization.

He was dreaming big and owning that vision of his company. How did he do this? We created this vision together and he had my support. I stood shoulder-to-shoulder with him as he created systems based on his values, shared his vision for the company with his employees, and integrated himself more firmly as an

Integrated Leader as the company excelled and continued to grow. He could always see it in his mind and feel it strongly in his body. Carrying the vision and continually feeling the glory of the experience as he let it echo through him. Being driven by his inner vision was the very key to manifesting on a daily basis.

Bringing families together was one of the strongest things that Jason wanted for himself and his legacy. Together, we looked at how bringing families more closely together might work, both in his family as well as his organization. Multiple generations of his entire family participated. He looked at the legacy within the family that was the legacy and inheritance from generation to generation. He had a profound vision of speaking and writing about that to the world—the inspired place of being a man on a mission bringing families together. He then made a conscious decision to go out and make an impact on the world, bringing families more closely together across the planet.

Physical

In his physical quadrant, Jason trained in boxing as well as worked out lifting weights at the gym. What was the area of his body that he chose to really challenge himself? As with a lot of my clients, it was lung capacity and endurance. Jason first had run half a mile, then a mile—but never further. The vision he developed was to run a half marathon, thirteen miles, within six months. His vision was crossing that finish line and experience the feeling of accomplishing something that his mind has told him "You can't."

Relationships

In terms of relationships, Jason's vision was to connect in an authentic and open manner. He had a great desire to connect more deeply and regularly with his family and friends and to create a loving relationship with a woman partner.

For Jason, being in a deep connected relationship with a woman was one of the hardest things he could imagine. It was truly frightening. He decided to challenge himself by beginning by connecting more authentically with his four boys, his friends, and all of the women he encountered. His vision was to be open and available to genuinely relate to them all, making himself vulnerable, spending time connecting with everyone in his life that he truly cared about.

Spiritual

For his spirituality quadrant, Jason vision was to develop a consistent daily spiritual practice that he could deeply feel and connect with his inner core. He wanted to listen on a deeper level and trust his Inner Knowing.

PART TWO
CHAPTER FIFTEEN

The Samurai: Strategy

Filled with the awareness of the Monk in self-understanding and the Sage in the vision, we next move to the Samurai pillar for action steps. Working together, I help you understand and discover how to manifest your vision one step at a time.

When you are integrated in self-wholeness and your vision is clear and resonates in your heart and soul and you listen to your Inner Wisdom, strategies seem to create themselves. Structure then becomes something that does not feel imposed from outside, but is simply inevitable. Small action steps become in alignment with your vision. You commit to not letting fear and resistance hold you back from manifesting your vision. You commit to implementing these Samurai strategies in all four areas: work/legacy, physical, relationship, and spiritual.

Within this pillar, it is important to remain aware of three areas in your body, thinking and feelings and your gut core wisdom (intuition). Listening carefully to all three areas will inform the strategies to manifest your visions. As your journey unfolds, you may find that the parameters and substance of your vision transforms into something different from what you had previously thought as your creation unfolds within the context of the experiences of your daily life. That is the process of living the vision in the immediate. Now rather than it being the end goal, you are living in the future. This allows you to listen to your core inner wisdom, mind and heart for the best steps to take and to let your vision evolve.

As the Monk, you understand your core beliefs and what beliefs will limit your true potential. The Sage creates your vision far beyond what you had imagined with no constraints by holding the images of completion in your own mind and heart.

In the Samurai pillar, you show up to challenge yourself in all areas of your life, to listen deeply using your mind, heart and gut to create the detailed strategies necessary and required to solidify your vision across the quadrants. In this pillar, you take the small, incremental practical steps that are easy to grasp and put into your life.

1. What is the one action that you can take to make your work vision happen more efficiently?

2. What one action a day can you do physically to move your body more efficiently, with good self-care?

3. What one action can you do today that can help you build or deepen your relationships?

4. What one action will move you into deeper connection to your gut instinct, your Higher Power?

The integration of the Monk and the Sage actually gives birth to the Samurai who gives guidance to the actions that will change your life forever. The Monk and the Sage in alignment create the doorway for the Samurai. The Samurai asks "What strategies am I going to create to manifest my vision and manifest different opportunities in my life?" We work together to create these strategies coming from the place where the vision is already here Now. How would you live in the present from the experience of your vision?

Work/Legacy

What is the next step you can take to manifest your work vision Now? Who do you need to call today? What information do you need to move forward? How do you connect with your employees to help them own their full potential and work toward the company vision? How do you create the structure of your business to manifest your vision? How would you show up in your organization? What small step can you take toward your legacy vision?

Physical

What is a small step you can take to improve your physical health and move toward your vision? Set aside even 15 minutes daily for exercise, stretching, yoga, taking a walk, training for a marathon, drinking more water or eating a healthier meal.

Relationships

What is the small step you can do to create better relationships—such as make a phone call, show gratitude, tell your partner you love them, or set time to be with your children? What can you do to further your highest ideal relationship vision?

The key question I ask is: how well do you listen to other people? I sometimes cite the 80/20 rule: 20% of what you do gives you 80% of the results you get. To deepen all of your relationships, listen 80% of the time and only talk 20% of the time. Ask questions, stay interested in the other people in your life, and actively listen to other people, repeating back to them what they've actually said, felt and expressed.

Spiritual

How can you connect to your core inner knowing? Meditation, starting at five minutes a day, prayer, walking in nature, sitting quietly, reading inspirational passage are some suggestions.

Write down these things that you intend to do each day to move yourself in all four quadrants toward your vision. Then, insert yourself into the vision completely, totally present and connected. Open yourself fully to having a true and real relationship with your staff or children, with your body, and your inner knowing. Let that strategy unfold while staying really focused on each of the small steps that are creating the outcomes you desire.

One of the strongest tools for creating strategies is developing structure around your daily activities. One way is to organize a morning routine is to include your visioning, your spiritual practice, and your body self-care. Those three areas will become your regular routine that doesn't shift. Once you start doing it every day, it will become automatic. You won't even have to think about it.

I get up at 4:00 in the morning to meditate. I work with my body with exercise and stretching, then do my reading and writing. I go over my visions. That is my solid routine. It's unwavering. I do it on a daily basis, and I don't ever question it. I follow the slogan that says, "Just do it."

My own experience as an entrepreneur was always to dive deeply into each new adventure, putting my everything into creating it. I always wanted to engulf myself in it. Having a regular daily spiritual practice, taking care of myself physically and being in healthy relationship with others helped keep everything growing together in balance and my business grew. Having an integrated life has influenced all areas of my life.

The Samurai is where you bring your learning experiences of the Monk and Sage into action and share your vision and mission with others through your actions. How you live, work, love and teach in your own life is a living example of what you bring to everyone around you, challenging yourself and all others to strive toward a higher standard in all areas.

PART TWO
CHAPTER SIXTEEN

Jason and The Samurai

Work/Legacy

Jason brought his values of people, service and integrity into his vision for his company. He started holding weekly meetings, really checking in with his staff, listening to their needs and encouraging feedback without being defensive. This, in turn, empowered his employees to be their best and do their best for the company because they felt more connected. He assigned himself the job of being an inspiration and leading by example. He started living his work vision by every day listening to the next step to exponentially help his business to grow with a firm foundation of structure and employees.

Jason's legacy work started at home. He made a point of regularly bringing his family together. He made it a priority. He shared with them what it meant to him to be bringing families together. Then he took these lessons back to his workplace, prompting his employees to bring their families together by listening and sharing their personal lives.

Physical

As he tied his shoes every day to go out to run, Jason's mind (his resistance) would tell him not to go, that he was not a runner. He had to constantly challenge his thinking and mindset about how he needed to show up to train in an area that was uncomfortable for him. Besides still going to the gym and working out, he would work every day on his challenge of running a half marathon, going a little further each day.

Relationships

A truly integrated vision of yourself really begins in the realm of relationships. Jason started by deeply re-connecting with his four boys. He started being the real father they had needed and wanted for a long time. Then he incorporated his parents and brothers. He made the effort to connect and really be in relationship with them all. In this way he started bringing his family together. He started connecting with his mother even though he had never had a deep or close connection with her before. Then he contacted family members that he had not contacted for a long time. He made frequent phone calls and took the time to keep connected with them all.

Spiritual

Jason started his spiritual practice with one minute a day, taking the time to breathe fully into the diaphragm, eyes open, eyes closed, devoting that one minute a day strictly for himself to connect to his gut and Inner Wisdom. He established that initial stretch as a way to go into his discomfort in a quadrant that he had never before explored.

He initially used this as a starting point to simply being present to his breath and his own energy, consciously focusing on his deep listening and returning his attention over and over to his breath when his attention wavered. He chose this strategy as something he could implement immediately without excuses, knowing he would and could expand the time.

PART TWO
CHAPTER SEVENTEEN

The Sensei: Integrated Leader

Forget safety. Live where you fear to live.
Destroy your reputation. Be notorious.

Rumi

In the Sensei pillar we will explore how you live as an Integrated Leader. How do you daily integrate your work/legacy, your physical, relationships and spiritual quadrants? I help you to continue to integrate and examine your Monk, Sage, and Samurai pillars within the Sensei so that you continue to grow and expand in all areas of your life. We will explore living in integrity with your goals and visions, and examine how you teach, promote and encourage others to live from their most authentic self and highest vision.

Work/Legacy

Are you inspiring and uplifting your employees and clients to live up to their highest potential? Are you empowering them to take on more leadership and live their highest dreams? Are you

THE SENSEI

manifesting your vision and taking the actions that are congruent in your life as an Integrated Leader?

What is your message, your voice, your mission and legacy? Are you living from a mission of service and sharing your mission with others? Are you making a difference to those around you and to the planet?

Physical

How are you modeling physical self-care? Are you taking time to nurture your body and to challenge yourself by living into your edge? Are you living your self-care?

Relationships

Are you being vulnerable and transparent in your relationships? Are you spending quality time with those you love? Are you opening yourself up to receiving as well as giving?

Spiritual

What words and actions do you choose to express your lived experience of your spirituality? How are you listening to your inner voice and then implementing those lessons in your life?

In the Sensei Pillar, we work on leading by example and empowering. Other individuals may learn from and be inspired by everything you have explored from the Monk, Sage, and Samurai quadrants. The Sensei teaches by example and continues to be actively creative through the process. Staying consistently on the path is being the Sensei!

The Sensei's job is to share what you are actually doing, how you are living and modeling that through all four quadrants in of your life. "Walking your talk" is my favorite way of expressing this. Integrity means that your word and actions are in alignment. You do what you say you are going to do.

The Sensei models how you live by consistently showing up with integrity and authenticity. As you move through the Sensei Pillar, you will start to see what areas you are not showing up or not challenging yourself. This is where we use the other pillars in accountability to continue to live as a conscious Integrated Leader.

As you begin to feel that you are implementing the Monk, Sage and Samurai Pillars, your old core beliefs might say:

"I am busy to meditate this week!"

"I didn't take good care of my body because I was traveling."

"I didn't have any time for my kids or my relationship. I didn't even bother to go into the office. I just let the employees handle it. They're doing just fine."

"I don't need to work on my legacy. My mission doesn't really matter. It takes too much time. I'm too busy!"

You may tell yourself stories that create a veil over your awareness that says, "I don't need to do this or that now. I'm just fine." When these thoughts come up, in the Sensei pillar, we re-examine the core thoughts coming up. Those beliefs that need the work or the focus of attention will then become highlighted. This is the pillar where working together is so necessary as consistent integration really become most important.

By having a mentor stand shoulder-to-shoulder with you to hold your vision, as I do with my clients, the areas that need continual work don't just fall away. By being accountable with yourself, shadows cannot come in and linger, building into greater intensity and hijacking your progress. You want a working partner in your plan, to encouraged you to work persistently and consistently on all these areas simultaneously. You will feel empowered and experience yourself as an Integrated Leader, who shows up with a presence of being whole and who is working on yourself constantly—and making money at the same time.

You may be someone who has always known that you wanted to make a lot of money; but in the process of that intense focus, you may have neglected taking care of your body or ignored important relationship, or your spiritual practice fell by the wayside, perhaps saying you would get to "later." You are now on a mission. You are focusing on your work/legacy, your very best self-care, meaningful personal and business relationships, and your spirituality. You are listening to your inner wisdom, experiencing your life as a whole person as an Integrated Leader, sharing a living empowerment with others by the example of both your words and deeds.

THE JOURNEY

Part Three

PART THREE
CHAPTER EIGHTEEN

Bruce's Story

The Vegan Revolutionary

Bruce was one of the most interesting entrepreneurial people I've worked with. He had been an architect and entrepreneur for over twenty years when we met. He was a strong visionary. Bruce had designed some of the most exquisite houses and buildings in New Zealand. Many opened with red velvet ribbon ceremonies acknowledging his design work. He was CEO of his own architectural design firm that was supervising a team of twenty people.

Reeling from the economic crash of 2008, he decided to take a look at his work and business. He realized that he had lost the driving passion that had always motivated him to excel in business. He decided to move away from architecture, and to take a year-long, around-the-world trip with his wife and three children. They travelled to more than twelve different countries simply to experience diverse cultures, living in and from a place of adventure, challenge and service, breaking the mold that he'd lived in for more than twenty years.

He realized that he wanted to have a mission-based company that would make a positive impact on the planet. He set out to create a business that was more in alignment with his personal beliefs. He himself ate only plant-based foods, and decided to implement his belief that a vegan-based diet was of supreme importance for the planet.

Investigating the possibility of being a part of an organization that would have a global impact through healthy vegan food habits, he became involved with a vegan alternative fast-food franchise company in Australia. It had been described as the "McDonald's of vegan food." When Bruce researched the company, its values and mission, he felt aligned with them, and invested in it, deciding to bring to bring a branch of it to New Zealand.

I have personally dined there with my children and we were excited to taste their offerings. Their "burgers," "chicken nuggets," even their "fish" tasted like their animal counterparts—even though everything in this restaurant was totally vegan.

He and his wife initially opened two locations following their vision of being a mission-based family and company, working together as a couple. They explored and created not only a plant-based company, but also a vegan fast-food culture unlike anything that had ever been seen before. I have been very impressed that they managed to develop a high-level culture in their company that has imbued values beyond the simple serving of food. They have deeply invested in their care and concern for their employees as well. When their employees serve the food, they also serve the energy infused into it by every member of the company of genuine love, care and concern for healthy food and vitality.

In one year, they opened these two restaurants and created gross revenue in each location that proved the worth of their visioning. Within that year, they brought their gifts as entrepreneurs to manifest their vision and had an enormous impact.

Bruce came to me with the intention and vision of wanting to open new stores in the UK and New Zealand. He realized he was not fully invested in his own approaches and strategies for manifesting this vision. He wanted and knew the value of coaching, and the kind of shoulder-to-shoulder support I could provide.

Within the Dojo, we applied the energies of the Monk, Sage, Samurai and Sensei in all the quadrants of his life. As he became clearer in his core beliefs, vision, strategy and actions, he began to change his life. I will now share with you his work in the Dojo in the Sage, Samurai, and Sensei pillars.

SAGE

We focused on his owning and expanding the vision of his business operations as a vegan alternative fast-food franchise company. Bruce envisioned me flying to London, where he is standing in front of his seventh location, waiting for me to arrive. He sees me coming towards him and he remembers that we talked about this vision. He experiences how we would look, how we would feel, the smell of the air, the clouds in the sky, all of the scents from the trees and the town. We created a vision of the success as if his vision had already happened. As I walk up, I give him a big hug, and then stand back and look at him. He feels the energy in his body and tells me "It's happened. I actually did it. There are seven locations here in London." He became fully invested in that vision.

Bruce could see the vision very clearly in his mind and feel it in his body. He knew it as already done, already completed. He knew it not as a place to get to, but a place to come from on a daily basis. By feeling the feelings in his body, he was able to show up in a radically different way than if he were to think, "I'm going to get there one day."

The energy is seen and felt RIGHT NOW. It is not in the future.

Working together in the Sage pillar, we moved through this process together, the vision became bigger and bigger. He was then able to vision and dream of what it was like to open hundreds and hundreds of locations in the UK and the possibility of going into India. He then expanded his vision and efforts out into a global vision of opening hundreds, even thousands, of stores all around the world. He saw the possibility of being bigger than McDonald's. He knew that his vision was his driving force and was the place from, not just the place to go. He visioned creating a legacy that would have a massive impact on the planet. He "saw" himself showing up as the man who created this vision as an Integrated Leader in all the arenas of his life.

Each step forward gave him more energy, opening up newer and bigger dreams and visions. This, in turn, fed his ability to practice on a daily basis seeing and feeling his vision unfolding into manifestation. This big vision allowed him to bring daily changes into his work, his own body, his relationships with others and his spiritual practice.

The treasures of that vision allowed him to apply his focus to his current location and the ones to come. He "saw" it all the way to the smallest detailed step, that one step moving the vision closer to being a reality daily. By consistently seeing and feeling it, it set the tone for how he showed up.

As a partner in this process, I held the vision with him. I became like the lead rider in a bicycle race, holding the pace and cutting through the wind resistance of any and all beliefs that may have been holding him back.

SAMURAI

As Bruce moved closer to owning his world vision, the strategy started to manifest naturally. He knew he needed more funding and investors to come aboard to create that vision. He started exploring the kind of investors he wanted who would share and support that same vision of having an enormous impact on the planet.

Soon, other opportunities started to manifest. Three new locations appeared miraculously in New Zealand. Then he got an offer to partially buy-in to one of his locations.

I'll never forget the call we had when I had said, "Who would be that investor who could actually make that deep level of impact on the planet? It would have to be somebody who has the same vision, the same desire for legacy that you have, and who has the same drive and passion for plant-based food."

I challenged him when he said, "I don't really know of anybody. I'm just not sure." I then asked, "Are you open to the possibility that that person is out there, just waiting for you to reach out to them?"

He committed to beginning to investigate who that person might be. By the following week, he had come to me and said, "I've done some research and have found a few people. This one person, a sheik, has the same vision and passion. His mission is to impact the planet through plant-based food."

On a coaching call, Bruce produced a picture of the man in question. I asked, "Who do you know that could introduce you, or who knows the sheik?"

He responded, "I don't know anybody over there."

I asked again, "Are you open to that happening?" I counseled him to allow the vision of the Sage to become reality simply by imagining knowing the person who could connect him with the sheik.

I suggested that it was his job to start reaching out to people. I told him "Who do you know that might know somebody who could connect you with the sheik?"

On our next call, we talked about it some more. He told me, "One of my cousins actually works in the same country where the sheik lives." It hadn't occurred to him previously because he hadn't talked to his cousin in a long time.

Bruce again committed to take the next step, and reached out to his cousin to ask if he knew anybody who might know the sheik.

On our next call, he reported, "You're not going to believe this. My cousin actually knows somebody that knows the sheik. He said that he'd be open to doing an introduction."

"Awesome! Let's see what that would look like," I responded. He called his cousin who said, "I'd be open to introducing you to him, but the vision of seven stores is too small for this type of person. We need to go bigger and write out a proposal that would interest him, challenge him to look at what it's like to make this kind of impact on the planet."

I loved that because that was completely in alignment with Bruce's vision. A bigger Vision!

Over the next few months, Bruce and his cousin put together a package for forty stores. He presented it to his friend who in turn presented it to the organization involved with the sheik. Soon after that, Bruce got the opportunity to speak with the gatekeeper for the sheik. They allowed Bruce to make the critical phone call to present that massive proposal.

I was in New Zealand teaching a workshop, when Bruce actually made that proposal. Bruce did not get the buy-in on the proposal, but he remembered that the vision is not the goal, but a place from which to come. We celebrated his "No" as a step to clarify his vision and implement the next step. He chose to listen to each step, to each "No" as an opportunity to hear what might be the next step, the next opportunity to lean into. Just making the proposal raised his confidence and helped him become clearer on his Vision.

SENSEI

His work in the Samurai pillar was to create the strategies and take the action steps that would propel his vision of making an impact on the planet.

In the Sensei pillar, Bruce is now really owning being an Integrated Leader, and making an impact in his spiritual practice, his self-care, his relationships and his legacy/work. He's now actively creating and owning all of who he is, and learning to do it in a balanced and healthy way. He continues to grow his business, expanding his store locations. He is also active being in relationships both as a father and a lover. He has become someone who honors and takes care of himself; as someone who listens to, and is guided by, his inner knowing. His journey continues.

PART THREE
CHAPTER NINETEEN

John's Story

Whatever it Takes

John has made millions of dollars as an entrepreneur in consulting and sales. He had an all-internet-based business. He's traveled the world, lived in different countries, and was married to his life partner for over 15 years.

We'd worked together, took a break, and then worked together again. We keep taking his journey together by expanding and exploring what it is to continually live into his potential and capacity as an entrepreneur. John is one of those men who resists and then goes, resists again and then goes some more. He continually challenges himself despite his resistance to it. It has been a very powerful journey that we've been on together.

John had a completely different challenge. He was making a great deal of money, but he didn't feel personally fulfilled, or a good enough person. John was living from an "I'm not good enough; I don't have enough," scarcity. His wife said, "He's the only one who doesn't know he's rich."

He strongly desired to learn to live from his heart and his gut, rather than from the dictates of his mind. He was living from an almost totally mental place, believing what his mind was constantly telling him. Many people believe that their thoughts are "reality" and that the inner critic is not only in charge, but is, in fact, correct. Some people call it living in your ego, or living from your thinking, not trusting your inner wisdom and feelings.

John worked harder than almost anybody I knew. He put in so much time working that he never really took breaks or vacations. When we met, he hadn't had a vacation in many years. He constantly felt the need to work all the time. He never had enough. His scarcity mindset led him to believe he was going "to lose it all." He brought a partner into his company, a man he believed would help the company grow. Then, even though the company was thriving and his new partner and employees were doing an amazing job, he continued to still slight himself, and still ran the limiting beliefs that, "I've got to do more. I will never work hard enough."

Another aspect of his dysfunctional approach was his inability to connect deeply with his life-partner. He never seemed to have time to connect with her, even when they lived together in other countries. He was constantly on the telephone and was constantly checking the internet. From the moment he woke up, he was filled with negative self-talk, cluttering his mind and coloring his conversations and interactions with her and everyone else.

John made a huge and very vulnerable decision when he and I started working together. He chose to enter the Dojo, that brutally honest place of practice, and leave his ego at the door. When he stepped onto the mat, he chose not to hide or hold anything back. He was committed to doing whatever it took to get what he needed—he wanted to live as an Integrated Leader.

We worked through the process of the Four Pillars: Monk, Sage, Samurai, and Sensei. We've been through these several times and we will constantly return to them to refine and dream bigger.

Work/Legacy

In the Monk pillar, John started paying attention to his business partner as a deeper reflection of himself. He saw his business partner as abrupt, confrontational, and not appreciative. Interacting with him has allowed John to receive critical feedback about his own communications style and how he was presenting himself. He made a conscious decision to show up in a much more authentic, honest, open, and vulnerable way.

He examined all of the old beliefs that had driven him for so long and asked, "Do I hold value in this new way of being? Can I align myself from this new place of awareness?"

John inspired me with his commitment and willingness to grow. He adopted the motto: "Discomfort is the new comfortable." Even though his mind occasionally insisted otherwise, he remained steadfastly convinced by his inner knowing. I stood shoulder-to-shoulder with him, encouraging and supporting his leadership as he shifted through his old beliefs in order to embrace his new ways.

In the Sage pillar, we visioned creating the exact company that was in alignment with his core values, manifested out of fullness, not scarcity; erected from trust and love in and for himself. He wanted an organization that would thrive and grow organically on a consistent basis.

His vision was a team of fifty people working in harmony and alignment to create his vision, manifesting it with positivity, and honoring each other's personal space and contribution to the greater whole. He saw and wanted a company infused with creativity and fun, brimming with opportunities, abundance and balance. I challenged him to get a clear and descriptive vision in his mind, and feel it in his body, knowing that the vision was his purpose and power. As John moved into the Samurai, the strategy started creating itself. Counter to what he had previously thought, John was actually motivated to slow down and listen to his gut instinct. As a result of that, it became clear that it was time to end his business partnership. He was inspired to create a new web site, company description and mission statement— all as a result of being more honest, slowing down and creating more abundance from this healthier place.

John started living his every day like a man on a mission, encouraging everyone he encountered to live more fully, honestly and authentically. He seems to show up in people's lives when they least expect it, and be with them when they need it. He believes that his support and love for others impacts their lives positively and tremendously influences how they show up in the world.

John extends himself to men and women in ways he is not

necessarily always aware. He acts completely natural, without any overarching agendas. He is so much on purpose, so mission-driven, that it's easy for him to support others. Now that he is paying better attention and taking better care of himself, he is able to value himself as an Integrated Leader.

He continues working on developing his leadership skills and the way he works with others. He practices his philanthropy and his personal money give-away. He made a conscious choice to expand his mission, to lean even more into it and honor his gifts and the impact that he is making in the world.

Physical

John really struggled to commit to going to the gym three days a week and he hated the thought of working out. So, he thought that my suggestion that working out would actually benefit his company was "crazy." Though he affirmed that going to the gym was "good for him," he had resisted committing himself because he "didn't have time," or he was "not worth it." His mind even came up with "It doesn't have any value for me—I just need to make more money." He was often assailed by his mind that asserted that he "needed to get on his email and write another proposal."

But then he began to see taking self-care time as small steps toward a greater wholeness, as opportunities to simply be and improve himself. He then chose to go to the gym daily to honor his body and to affirm to himself that he was worthy of making a lifetime commitment to himself and to his body. It was simply a matter of taking one small step and then another, always moving forward.

Relationships

John had not acted on opportunities to deeply connect with his wife or his family for a very long time. He had a bad habit of taking his phone with him everywhere. On vacation with his wife, he struggled to leave it in another room. After our first three months of working together with his new awareness, he booked a three-week vacation to Italy with his wife. He actually took the opportunity to set aside a full ten days for them to simply enjoy themselves.

Spiritual

John's orientation to listening to his mind chatter and especially the Inner Critic led him to never having a relationship with his still, Inner Voice. He came to me to help him redefine himself as a larger, more complete and more integrated person.

Working together, we created a plan that would challenge his thinking, so that he would start to trust his body wisdom and his gut knowing. One constant challenge for him was to wake up in the morning and meditate. We started his practice with one minute a day. He started experiencing the tremendous benefits of meditation and started taking time every morning to sit quietly within himself.

I personally believe that all entrepreneurs are only living at about fifty-percent of their potential and capacity. Leaning into your self-created limitations edge is truly enriching for the Integrated Leader. It is a continuing practice with rewards in all four quadrants of your life.

PART THREE
CHAPTER TWENTY

Renée's Story

Raising Leaders

Renée and I have known each other for over twelve years. I originally started working with her son to help develop his purpose and passion.

Four years ago, she decided it was time for us to work together on her legacy/work. She had been running and operating The Still & Moving Center that she and her husband had founded seven years before. She had been questioning whether to continue moving forward with that work or to let it go. She is also the President of her family-owned construction company that is thriving.

MONK

In the Monk pillar, Renée and I took a deep dive into her core beliefs and how she had set up the organization. It immediately became clear that her senior staff were very dependent on her to run the Center. She never seemed to have time for herself and her family. Neither did she seem to have space to vision and expand even more. It was as if she were starving for air to breathe. We looked at how she was showing up in her life and her core beliefs that she held to limit her self-care, her need to take care of others and her inability to have time to vision and expand what she wanted. She acknowledged that she was "100% responsible for what she had created at the Center, and would not let her fears get in the way."

SAGE

Renée is a phenomenal visionary. She sees and manifests like very few others I have ever met. When she creates the appropriate space and time for herself to do so, visioning comes very naturally for her as she connects to her body and deep listening. In doing so, she created a vision as somewhere to come from, not somewhere to go. This process activates her mind and body simultaneously to show up as the Integrated Leader with a vision in each quadrant of her life.

It was all very exciting and frightening at the same time when we generated a vision of creating a worldwide organization with teachers and instructors from all around the world. We started our journey, intentionally creating a vision of the kind, type and quality of staff and support that would take the Center to the next level, and allow her to be closer to her family, as she was soon to become a grandmother.

SAMURAI

When her Monk and Sage were both operating and integrating together, the action became immediately clear. She began by creating the space for herself to spend time in her "teahouse," to connect and listen to her body deeply.

As she started owning her power more deeply, she began giving more responsibility to her staff. It created a disruption in the organization and the staff who weren't in alignment with her choice to stand in her power and own who she really was. Those who were not in attunement quickly left. We found that it was sometimes necessary to break things down in order rebuild a more efficient and growing organization.

SENSEI

As Renée and I explored Sensei pillar energy, it brought out a whole new level of her leadership in her organization. Her mission had always been to bring out the magnificence in others. This sterling quality became the primary focus of her leadership. I have been gifted the opportunity of leading her team through the journey of creating their own vision, one that they can own in their bodies and minds as an ultimate place to create from. She, in turn, supports each and every one of her team to follow their own passions and dreams. Ultimately, she found that it is to the benefit of the whole organization to empower her employees.

During the more than three years we have worked together, we are continually visioning and creating not only current projects, but implementing the continuing expanding vision of all that she has dreamed was possible and more.

PART THREE
CHAPTER TWENTY-ONE

Michael's Story

A VIP Weekend

Michael and I went to Maui for a three-day, one-on-one intensive to allow him to push his edge, expand his mindset and access that other sixty percent he knew he had that was hidden inside of him. The process began the moment we got in the car to drive to the airport in Kona. I could feel his tension in my body, and knew he absolutely had to trust me and let go of it.

Day 1: The Uji (Letting Go into the Flow): Zip-lining in Haiku.

We started off with an opening ceremony. We used ceremonial sage to smudge away any lingering ego impulses; set intentions for the day. We did a five-minute meditation to integrate the intentions more fully in our bodies. Then we journeyed to the largest zip lines in Hawaii.

As we drove to the site, we explored what it was that made him happy on the inside and on the outside, living in ways that made him feel fulfilled. Then, we investigated what was holding him back from letting go of control, from allowing himself to simply feel his feelings, to be truly OK to have his "specialness" without having to defend it, and to connect more deeply with his wife.

By the time we arrived at the base of the mountain, the energy was still building. There were eight different zip lines, and the top one was just a little speck far away at the summit of the mountain. As we approached each one, he set an intention for what he wanted and named what he was going to have to let go of in order to achieve that intention. Then he made a conscious decision to let go of it. By the time we completed the entire series, I could feel his renewed energy and openness. During the evening session, the floodgates of creativity and possibility opened for him. We explored how his life might be if the vision he was designing was the actual circumstances of his life right now with new and more fulfilling connections and relationships. His dreaming was so big, he thought he might not be able to complete it in his lifetime. We finished the day with a closing ceremony and meditation around that dream, visualizing and anchoring it in his body, and finally ended with a closing five-minute meditation.

Day 2: Diving into the Depth of the Core: (Gut Instinct) Free diving around the Island of Lanai.

We opened the day on the drive to the boat by designing a customized daily spiritual practice and ceremony. Sitting quietly and breathing into his Core (Gut), and exploring that deep, intimate personal relationship with himself, I had him give me examples of listening to his Core and how it supported him. Then we got on the boat and headed to Lanai. The wind was blowing and the water was splashing on our bodies. The energy kept building with our anticipation of exploring the unknown. Our first stop was about a hundred yards out from the island. We stopped at a white sand beach with no one else on it. The captain gave us the option to swim to the beach and explore. Michael was the first one in the water. I was right behind him. It felt like his inner kid came out to play as we swam to the beach. When we felt the warm sand between our toes, the only footprints in the sand were our own. We had a long discussion about the difference between his mind, his body, his heart, and his Core and the importance of using them separately and together.

We continued around the island to our first dive site. Going underwater and holding our breath gave us the opportunity to watch the landscape of our mind unfold as we swam. When you are holding your breath, the mind will often tell you that, "You're out of oxygen and you have to come up for air or you will die." (We had actually used less than forty percent of what was available.) We just had to trust our bodies and not react to the fear the mind was generating.

We did three different dives that day. The colors of the corals under the water were so bright and extraordinary, filled with many different species of unbelievable fish of every description. The water was so clear that we could see at least fifty yards out. On our third dive, the water at the surface started getting rough. As we dove down, a remarkable calmness developed, a stillness that filled his body. It was extremely peaceful, a perfect metaphor to describe how the mind can be rough and moving on the surface while the Core remains calm and peaceful.

The final hour ride back to Maui was one of the roughest rides I have ever had. We were all wearing full rain gear and were still getting constantly drenched with water. We had to hold onto the boat rails so that we didn't simply fly out. We all stayed focused on breathing into our bellies, maintaining our calm and focusing with purposeful intention. Michael said he experienced a place of calmness that he knew he could return to.

That night we refined Michael's custom-made spiritual practice, assuring that he would retain what he had learned and be able to return to it on a daily basis. Developing this kind of Core training is very similar to muscle training—consistent practice leads to greater strength and agility.

Day 3: Visioning what's next: See it and feel it.
Waterfall hike and the Seven Sacred Pools.

Going out into nature and hiking is a great way to stimulate creativity. The next day, we explored the absolute beauty of Nature while exploring his dreams and visions for the future. We worked on what would bring him maximum fulfillment, while serving and uplifting others. He stated that he wanted to create companies and other organizations that would serve the entire planet.

We hiked through a massive bamboo forest and he shared about his life journey growing up. We explored the life lessons and beliefs that he had carried forward into his life. We arrived at the seventh pool and watched in awe as a fifty-foot waterfall poured into it. We used the setting to share an amazing purification and renewal ceremony dedicated to what he was creating as a vision for his future.

It has been a joy and an honor to watch him move and shift his companies to be in alignment with his mission and begin having a global impact on men, women and children all around the world.

ALCHEMY

Part Four

PART FOUR
CHAPTER TWENTY-TWO

LIFE LESSONS

Put communities and clients you work with at the center of your thoughts, plans, and actions in all you do, work with people, not for them.

Jackie Lyles, "Transformational Growth"

My Why

Remembering the reason and the why for what you are doing is very important. The reason you invite any client into your life is your "why." I choose clients that I feel connected to. I base my "why" on the most effective working relationship. I want to help my clients change their lives and live as Integrated Leaders so that they can feel fulfilled in all areas of their life. I know that I can share deeply with this type of client and help them to develop a more productive and joyful life. That is my Why.

I always ask "How can the person I am working with best benefit from what I have to give?" I must have a sense that the client is someone I really want to work with, and I need to feel that I have the skills and the needed abilities to say, "Hey, let me show you my gifts so you can develop your gifts and experience them for yourself."

The more I am being me, presenting my authentic self, the more I can share from the place of my power, vulnerability and transparency. It is a very powerful lesson when my clients see me as completely available, transparent, and vulnerable. I've been told "Wow, you shared something with me that really showed me who you are." This models for my clients how to show up from their most vulnerable and transparent place.

Embracing your Fear

Fear can be a great tool to motivate you to think and create in ways that are beyond what you had previously thought possible. Generally, when people feel fear energy in their bodies, their first reaction is to shrink away from it in order to feel "safe." The key is to move toward your fear and understand it. Then use your fear to motivate you into dreaming bigger than you ever thought possible.

I had a client who had been an entrepreneur for over twenty years, and had created a very successful business. He had it all—at least on the outside. The big house, the cars, toys and a membership at the top country club. Things were very different for him on the inside. He did not feel fulfilled and was fearful of change. He believed he was doing everything that he thought he should in order to feel internally successful. But it was not the life he wanted and he knew it was time for a change. We started working together to lean in even closer to his edge and his fear of change. We took a deep dive inward and explored the roots of his fears. This process allowed him to take the next step to create the life he envisioned.

Bull Riding is like Being an Entrepreneur

Riding a bull is like being an entrepreneur, shifting your attention and balance frequently to stay synchronized with the will of a two-thousand-pound beast trying to throw you. You can either open yourself up to the amazing energy or you can try to fight and find yourself in the dust.

You can either get on, try to control and manipulate without a clear vision of the outcome you intend or you can allow yourself to open up and flow as if dancing with a great beast, creating structure, plans and visions so that you remain clear and present in any situation that arises.

I worked with a man who was a bull rider preparing to go to Nationals; but he was not completing his full eight-second ride he felt he needed to win. We explored his recent experiences and he observed that he had started trying to control the bull rather than relaxing and merging his awareness with it to create greater harmony. We used visualization exercises, with him feeling and seeing the successful completion in both his mind and body. Embracing this new harmony within himself, he became the very picture of an entrepreneur immersed in his own flow. Creating the structure, routine and vision allowed him to feel present in the Now and ride the bull instead of fighting the process.

Playing your Cards

I worked with a landscaping contractor who was struggling with finding the ultimate employee. He'd gone through twenty applicants before we started working together. I loved using the analogy of a deck of cards with him. How many cards are in a deck? Fifty-two, right? And how many aces are in that deck? Four? If you draw a card off the top, you have no idea what card you're going to get next. It could be an ace. You may have to go through a few cards to get one. But the willingness to go through the deck, looking for an ace, turning over all fifty-two cards if you have to, is what gets you your ace.

Going through those fifty-two cards is an expensive process. But every time you hire and let go of someone who doesn't work out, that's expensive too. Let's say that it costs twenty-thousand dollars to hire somebody, and train them and an equal amount to fire someone. So, you must be both vigilant and selective. Once, I almost went bankrupt hiring the wrong person. I invested three months in training a person for a position—and then he just walked away. When I found the right person, she worked out very well and we created great success together. Now I always help my clients pay close attention, listening with your mind, heart and gut, to hire your next ultimate employee.

PART FOUR
CHAPTER TWENTY-THREE

Transforming Limiting Beliefs

When I first heard the words "limiting beliefs," I immediately looked outwardly, hoping to see what it was that I actually believed. I originally believed that I needed to understand and destroy my old "internal" limiting beliefs and unproductive stories that I'd carried that were wanting to keep me safe.

In my personal journey, I discovered that my true edge lay in actually acknowledging the depth, breadth and real meaning of all of my life experiences. Owning my fears and concerns as if they were loved ones trying to protect me allowed me to go beyond the ordinary system of disowning aspects of my personality. This perspective has deeply enriched me personally, and allowed me to apply these principles to working with my clients in a positive, supportive way, filled with compassion and empathy. That is my edge right now. My business is really about coaching clients in new and better ways to see themselves and their beliefs in a totally different light in order to create the desired life they want to live. Now.

I have abandoned the entire idea of living "safely." Now I am leaning into where I had previously feared to live. I have learned not to fall into being overwhelmed by fear, and instead feel the excitement of the energy, riding that line, leaning into the fear and stimulation simultaneously.

One of my favorite analogies is that of the big wave surfer. Those who surf the big waves are a special breed. They watch for the next big wave, choosing to embrace the excitement and the "holy shit" feeling at the same time.

In our work together, I constantly challenge you to dream BIG, and to live your biggest dream by integrating your old limiting beliefs. We always have this internal sense of how things should be or could be. Integrating your old destructive beliefs is the exact thing that you need to do to go to the next level.

Releasing the memories of those old fears allows you to let go of the old and limiting beliefs and stories. Reflecting on an old story no longer as a victim opens the possibility of choosing in the present to live in joy and happiness—to continually show up in that place that embraces excitement and fear together.

I have discovered through my activities as an athlete and martial artist, that the body will always follow the head. So, if I am looking at my feet in a judo competition, that is likely where my body will end up. It's all about focus.

There's a big difference between intention and attention. If I make an intention to ride a big wave and put my attention on staying in the moment, simply tracking the field, I do not clutter up my attention by focusing on missing a wave or the possibility of falling.

I had long held the belief that I had to sacrifice my freedom, time and relationships in order to create my financial ideal for my business. When I looked back, I realized I had chosen that belief. I had falsely believed that I would create more time with my family, more freedom and better relationships, if and when I reached that far-flung financial goal. By creating such a huge gap between intention and attention and putting my attention on the envisioned future, I allowed myself to stop paying attention to the present. I was being driven by an old belief system that demanded that I sacrifice myself in the present for the imagined ideals of the future. When I reached my goal *then* I could be who I wanted to be.

It takes a great deal of self-examination to be aware of your limiting beliefs. Assessing what it is you really want can bring the understanding that you can create a belief to have everything you want without totally sacrificing yourself in the present. You can stop obsessing about the future by leaning into your deepest, oldest fears, including the limiting belief that you must sacrifice your freedom and relationships to achieve success.

Here's an example from my own life. One of my old beliefs was that I had to struggle to earn money. I had to work so hard all the time that I didn't have any energy for a life outside of work. It was a perfect set up for failure.

I actually used to believe that my choices were forever binding. For example, if I chose to snowboard, then I couldn't ski downhill with regular skis without compromising my skills in snowboarding. I had believed that these choices were unchangeable. Now I am far more flexible and know that I can change anything at any time.

My coach openly questioned my self-imposed false beliefs. He challenged me to work less and to take a vacation, something I had not done in years. I decided to relax and lean into my edge around this by taking positive action. I started working only two days a week, and took two full months off. During this time, I rewrote my limiting beliefs, created multiple six figure accounts and thoroughly enjoyed my beautiful wife and children. I instituted the new belief that I could have it all without carving deeply into other extremely important areas of my life.

The generative language I adopted was: "I am creating a five-million-dollar coaching practice. I have more money, time, freedom and fun than ever before; and my relationships are deeper than ever in my life." With that intention, I keep my attention in each moment in front of me, with each client and with everything I do in my life right Now.

When I hold a cherished vision and offer it as something I love, my clients benefit and it enriches their lives. However, with the vision comes action.

If I decide to "wait" for the clients I want to work with, I will stay in that waiting mode, saying, "I am waiting to create the perfect clients to walk in the door." Yet I cannot know who the perfect client is until I actually start opening myself up to individuals who might potentially be ideal. Otherwise, I'm just waiting, sitting in a void of non-action.

When you do the inward looking of the Monk, the vision work of the Sage and the action work of the Samurai, you will see significant changes to your old limiting beliefs and live as a Sensei as an Integrated Leader.

WRITING EXERCISE: Limiting Beliefs

Make a list of five beliefs that you hold that may be keeping you from living the expansive life you wish to live. What are some self-defeating systems you have in place in your life?

PART FOUR
CHAPTER TWENTY-FOUR

Turning Points

Carlos

When I was seventeen years old, I joined a regional occupational program through my high school. I wanted to get out of high school as quickly and easily as possible. I was dyslexic, with undiagnosed ADD and OCD. I thought differently than the other kids.

In this program, I spent ½-day in school and ½ day learning how to build and customize cars in the auto body shop. I thought to myself that I did not need to go to college and this would be an easy way out. From the first day in this program, I heard many people talking about how "wonderful" Carlos was. And I wondered, "Who is this guy?" I was jealous without even meeting him.

Carlos was a 6'1",180-pound, blond haired, blue eyed German. Everybody liked him. Except me. I worked at avoiding him. I worked at keeping my distance. I really didn't want to talk to him, except that we both had custom trucks we wanted to develop into show vehicles.

When we did connect, our relationship developed very rapidly, even though we were more competitors at first and not really instant friends. Three months later, he asked me to help him lower his Chevy S-10 pickup. We went over to his house after school, and his mother immediately welcomed me—offering me food and drinks. She genuinely cared. We worked on his truck for the next two hours. While taking the suspension apart, we immediately bonded over our shared dreams and visions about creating show trucks. That day marked our journey together as friends, colleagues, entrepreneurs, and later as partners in one of my biggest businesses, one that shaped my life as an entrepreneur. He not only could see my vision, he made it clear that he wanted to join me in manifesting it.

Before I was eighteen, we had completed the extensive transformation and entered my truck into our first car show. We took second place that year and made plans to get my truck into one of the high-class, national magazines. After that first show, we went to an event in Reno. A truck magazine photographer offered to feature my truck in their magazine. During the next three months, we entered my vision-truck into many car shows. When the magazine came out, my truck was the featured article when we took first.

LIFE LESSONS

The person who might first appear to be threatening may turn out to be your best friend and biggest supporter. Don't let your fears stop you.

Chuck

In 2000, I'd been doing business for over ten years. I had a very comfortable life—plenty of free time, and my business was thriving. But I was still deeply dissatisfied. Something deep inside me wouldn't let me rest. I knew the business had the potential to grow much bigger.

In 2000, I hired my first business coach, Chuck. Chuck and I went on a journey together over the next five years, creating two different businesses and steadily growing those through our regular meetings and coaching appointments. We set goals, and I met them week after week. My gross income tripled in less than two years, and continued to grow for the next three years after that. I was supremely impressed with the power of being supported by having a coach and by being held while I created my dreams and visions. It has been an essential part of my growth as an entrepreneur.

LIFE LESSONS

Having a business coach is priceless.

The Mankind Project

In 2008 I went to a weekend training that changed my life. This rite of passage (initiation) was sponsored by The Mankind Project. Prior to that weekend, my definition of, and the sense of power that I carried, was power over others. It was a superior edge I carried all the time, especially as a boss who could fire anyone any time if they disagreed with me. My attitude was that every one of them should be grateful to be working for me.

Through this leadership program, I learned what it was like to truly be a leader. I learned to redefine power as vulnerability coupled with transparency. I learned to meet individuals in their own space. I learned about being mutually supportive with others to bring out greatness. I took this knowledge and learned how to collaborate to build a business while still keeping a deep connection with the people I worked with. Understanding that I can increase profits and still maintain personal and professional growth is phenomenal.

Through doing my deep inner work, I have learned to model for other men and women the very qualities I find most beneficial and rewarding. Showing up vulnerable and powerful in my coaching and consulting practice, I help my clients in a powerful and yet extremely human way to do their own work as easily and deeply as possible.

LIFE LESSONS

Vulnerability and transparency are the essence of leadership.

PART FOUR
CHAPTER TWENTY-FIVE

Who Do You Know?

The year was 2006, and my business had grown from two employees to ten, with fifteen different divisions and ten subcontractors. I was now customizing and enhancing high-end cars (Ferraris, Austin Martins, Maseratis). You name it, we worked on it.

One of my accounts was San Francisco BMW and we were customizing thirty to fifty cars a month. Bruce was my main contact at the dealership. We still talk all the time and have become good friends. Bruce invited me to lunch and said he had someone he wanted to introduce me to. I didn't think much of it because all my connections were from one person introducing me to another. He said he had a surprise for me after lunch.

After lunch, we started driving towards San Francisco. We went to the Ferrari dealership. As we pulled into the driveway, I saw the red, orange and yellow Ferraris. I was like a kid in a candy store. I was so excited. I asked him, "What are we doing here?" He said, "I have someone for you to meet."

Walking through the Ferrari dealership the smell, the sights, sounds, and colors were amazing. I was in awe. As we walked in and he introduced me to the receptionist, he started walking towards the back offices. I felt my hesitation. Then he told me he was going to introduce me to the manager Kevin. The store was immaculate and spotless. There were Ferraris everywhere.

As I walked in, I shook Kevin's hand. Kevin said he wanted me to do all their work for aftermarket add-ons. Was I dreaming? My heart was pounding. My hands were sweating. All I could say was, "Yes, let's do it."

He said, "Sounds good. When can we drop off the first car?" Inside I was thinking holy shit!!! He said, "You will do all of our work." When I stood up, I said to Kevin, "You know we pick up and deliver."

He smiled and grabbed a set of keys to a 360 Challenge Stradale and tossed them to me. And he said, "I have 10 more cars for you when you're done with this one."

We walked into a warehouse full of about 50 cars. We walked up to a red, sexy beautiful Ferrari. Turning the key and pushing the buttons, the engine revved. I have never driven one of these cars before. It was a dream come true.

That day changed everything. Referrals from all over the US and Canada came in, not only for Ferraris but everything from Indy cars to fully custom rods.

LIFE LESSONS

1.   Relationships with everyone you meet are important. You never know who you are standing in front of.

2.   You have to be willing to ask for what you want and be clear.

3.   If it feels big and palm sweating, you are in the right place.

4.   Don't be afraid to ask for support. Always, at the end of a conversation with the customer, I say, "Word-of-mouth is my biggest seller. Who do you know who could use this? "

PART FOUR
CHAPTER TWENTY-SIX

Be Scared/Do it Anyway

Being uncomfortable drives me to operating at my best in all four quadrants. I examine where I'm holding myself back from having and expressing my voice and actions. When I allow fear and open myself to embrace it, I can work with the exact area that leads me to the greatest success in being an Integrated Leader, and to opening up to my goals at the next level.

When you come across situations in your life that are frightening, maybe even scare the hell out of you, I invite you to try leaning into these areas. Sign up for events or workshops that you have to train for or expend special effort to complete. Set a high intention and then go have fun.

For me, an example of this occurred in 1982 when I had placed first in a National Judo Tournament in Reno, Nevada. I was excited. I had trained long and hard for the competition.

I was then invited to compete in the 1984 Junior Olympics. I had no real idea what I was saying when I said, "Yes." I was told that the training would start immediately, even though it was two years away. It was a dream come true. Conversely, I was very scared.

The training alone was intense—weight training for two hours every day, followed by going straight to school and an after-school session. It was just not fun. I felt pushed harder and harder every single day. By the time the Junior Olympics came, all the fun was gone, but the experience training and the discomfort it generated gave new confidence and empowerment. As I got older, I recalled these experiences and applied their lessons in my businesses and in training for other events.

When I was 19 years old, I was opening my own first business and scared—but I pressed on. Through my experiences in the Olympics, I knew in myself that I was doing the right thing. I have since then succeeded and failed in business, always continuing to move forward. That is the key.

LIFE LESSON:

If there is a failure, use it to motivate yourself, and not see it as a loss, but simply as an experience you learn from.

PART FOUR
CHAPTER TWENTY-SEVEN

Soulful Work

Soulful work has a healthy narcissistic quality.
We see ourselves reflected in our work and we grow in
self-love as we see our work accepted, valued, and self-
transcendence. All three of these are necessary for work to
be soulful. Each contributes to the formation of character.
From a Buddhist point of view, the soul value of work depends
on whether or not it contributes to the purification of human
character.

John Johnshaw

For me, there are primarily two different kinds of work. There
are cash projects and there are soulful projects. Some projects
feel good and in alignment with my mission in life. They are my
passion and feed my soul immediately. My coaching practice
and working with people in the area of personal growth are
soulful projects that light me up. My cash work has been what
I have done so I could follow my passions and provide for my
family too. While I was in transition toward my soul's visions,
I have worked at creating new businesses in window tinting

and after-market products and customizing cars, and even construction work.

At one point, I came to the realization that my cash flow projects were not feeding my soul. I had to look at how my passion work could become my cash work until they united. Fortunately, my soul work usually fueled my cash work energetically so I could bring greater passion and enjoyment to my life and my cash work. I have worked with my vision and progressed now so that my passion work and my cash work are the same.

Initially, I took on clients in my coaching practice who really didn't motivate or inspire me. At one point, I had ten clients. It often felt like pulling teeth without anesthetic to get some of them enthused and stimulated. Now I am confident and experienced enough to take the time to carefully screen my clients in order to ensure that I get to work with people that can benefit most from our work together. I am exhilarated by my work. It is always exciting for me to see clients make real changes in their lives both professionally and personally. I know that I have helped them design and nurture this change. Understanding and incorporating the Integrated Leader has been an instrumental part of my client's success.

WRITING EXERCISE: What Feeds Your Soul

Make a list of what really stirs your passions, what feeds your soul. Don't edit yourself. Do not concern yourself with income or profit yet. That will come later. Allow yourself to write down everything that attracts you, no matter how obscure—even if you have never attempted it. Just write until you feel your list is complete. Let it rest for a little bit and then read through it carefully. Really look and feel what you have written. Imagine each of your choices and envision what might be entailed in each of them. Next, allow yourself to listen deeply to your inner urgings and put a passionate number by each of your choices. When you have done this, look it over again. Make sure that your choices really reflect what you are feeling. Then, look carefully at your list and go through it again, this time looking at income potentials (either in or related to your choices). For example, you might have writing as a passion choice. There are really very few top-notch professional writers, but you could potentially make a living being an editor or some other adjunct profession. This time, as you go through your list, put a number by each choice for income potential.

The idea here is to analyze your own passions and income potentials to find a perfect match that might exist. The higher the passion number and income number for each of your choices, the more likely you will have come to find your own unique niche for a top choice. The key here will be how you best merge your passion project that provides inspiration with a cash project that provides daily essentials.

You can sometimes do this list on a daily basis, asking yourself what are your top passion projects. Allow yourself to feel into them; and then balance them with income requirements to see if you're going to make them a top priority or not.

This is where Integrated Leadership, coaching with the Dojo, pillars, and quadrants is important. Make your soul work your cash work and get the help to turn that vision into reality.

LIFE LESSONS

1.   You can push yourself beyond what you think is possible.

2.   You may have to continue your cash work to take care of yourself and your family until you can manifest your soul work.

3.   You can move on and learn from what might appear as a loss.

4.   The more you show up the more you learn and grow.

5.   Working on all four quadrants is essential to turn your cash work into your soul work.

PART FOUR
CHAPTER TWENTY-EIGHT

Live in the Now

Is it possible that a human being can show up one hundred percent fully present, one hundred percent of the time? It's very unlikely. Given the many, many possibilities and all of the distractions, it is quite easy to move away from the moment.

On the other hand, I believe that it is certainly possible, and even required, that living in the moment is important to succeed. The key to the entire equation is practice. How do you practice living in the moment and trust yourself to take the next step toward your vision, making it a reality? Living in the moment does not mean you don't plan for the future. Living in the moment means you listen and take the next step in *this* moment to make your vision come true.

One of my main teachings is that at any moment you have the ability to shift your thinking, acting and being to a different frequency or to another level of awareness and action that is more personally satisfying and enriching to your life.

One of the biggest factors blocking this is fear. It is fear that stops your highest thoughts and action.

What difference would it make in your life if you stepped forward into your fears and acted in the best interests of yourself and others in the moment? Think of how much positive change you might make for yourself, your family and your loved ones. Practice in each moment to step into old (even cherished) fears; and then, embracing them momentarily, choose to step beyond them into a new and more desirable behavior or thought pattern. In our work we exam your fears and you choose and decide to try on new behavior. You are not asking yourself to "permanently change" anything. Just try on something new you choose to change at this moment.

My Personal Strategy

I have always wanted to achieve grand results. I believe that if I keep living in the moment and leaning into my fears, I can achieve the necessary shift to get the results that I want. It requires energy and concentration and it demands desire and attention. It is a relatively small amount of effort that is almost invisible. Yet a tiny shift changes everything, especially for individuals who are high performers and manifestors.

In spite of my positive intentions, I have had to acknowledge where I was unsuccessful and didn't have positive results. My strategy was that if I imagined the worst-case scenario in this moment, then I could decide whether the risk was worth it. When I was deciding whether to close my business down, my imagination worked with the possibility of Amber and I living in a tent. We talked it over. Once we looked at that, it led to a decision to open up more space and trust in our lives and to take that risk.

I have always had a fallback position. Since 1989, I have always known I could utilize my experience customizing and painting cars as an alternative resource if things went bad. Knowing that I have skills and job experience in other fields has allowed me to feel secure no matter what the circumstances. It has given me the confidence and strength to go forward, to just see what might transpire, to really lean into my edge and fully open to my fear and my one hundred percent potential.

Living Examples

In 2015 I was preparing to present a workshop called "Limitless Success Adventure" at Hapuna Beach Prince Hotel. Leading up to, and during the workshop, all my mental chatter came up, trying to dissuade me from going forward, telling me that I was not good enough, I wasn't doing enough, and I didn't have any value.

From all of my years of practice in facing my fears and limiting beliefs, I was able to experience and acknowledge them in the moment while staying present and focused on the task at hand.

I had another opportunity to look at my fear when I was in my Mastermind Group in 2011. A fellow group member told me I was only playing at fifty percent. I asked myself if that level of participation was serving me and was it serving the group? I realized that the way I was showing up in the group was how I was showing up outside of the group. My peers called me to step further into my greatness. They commented on my lack of presence, and asked, "Where were you? You're like halfway there. We want to see all of you."

It has now been eleven years since I received that feedback. Choosing to show up in the moment with awareness and openness has allowed my business to grow in revenue and my life to feel integrated and fulfilling. I am choosing to participate in my life at one hundred percent. Playing at one hundred percent, and showing up with my fullest potential in this moment totally resonates with me. The more I challenge myself to serve my clients and others in my life, the more I'm able to give and allow my one hundred percent to show up. I realize that I'm as perfect as I can be in this moment and I honor that.

PART FOUR
CHAPTER TWENTY-NINE

On My Journey

To this day, I continue to work with my own fears and resistance. I have had to work through many decades of beliefs that I thought were correct—only to find out, as I progressed along the path, that much of what I held sacred and fiercely protected was, in fact, only partially true.

My own mental beliefs have never prevented me from participating in what I thought was possible in sports but I found it to be more difficult in the other areas of my life. As I have taken on more and more challenges, I have come to discover what is called "disconfirming evidence." I have experienced evidence that proved to me personally that much of what I had taken to be "truth" was actually not true. I have developed a different relationship with my belief systems. I am now far more open and willing to investigate everything with a more child-like curiosity.

Four years ago, I ran a half-marathon because I like to do challenging activities. I did "Hell on the Hill" with Jesse Itzler, a race where you run up and down a huge hill one hundred times.

In my work, I challenged myself to dream bigger than I'd ever dreamed before, and to live into my edge of creating something seemingly impossible. Being a rebel and an outside-of-the-box thinker, I considered possibilities. "What would be the most challenging thing that I could do that would have an impact in this world as my legacy"?

My choice for my service and legacy was to create a school for dyslexic, ADD, and OCD kids. This was a huge stretch, especially since I myself have the super powers of being dyslexic and have ADD. I am able to hold a big vision; and I am capable of generating support in areas in which I'm not an expert. I never knew that carrying such a big vision and using it as a place to come from would take me on such a magical journey.

With this vision I have coached small school projects and facilitated a billion-dollar, multiple-schools project designed along the lines of the Sudbury School model that embraces student empowerment while designing their own education. Owning that I'm a change-maker in education and a disrupter of the way education-as-usual is presented, I take a stand that the educational system needs to be different. I can see it in my mind and feel it in my body. I envision myself standing in front of Congress presenting my approach as a new way of delivering education. I feel it in my body. It is exhilarating. It makes my palms sweaty and my knees quiver. I can feel it now, just imagining that place, a place to come from, not as a place to get to. It takes all of us to change the planet. We are the ones who came here to do it.

It is both staggering and incredible to me that I am taking on such a massive challenge. I will always strive to fulfill my life visions.

PART FOUR
CHAPTER THIRTY

Working with Pain

When the new knocks on your door, open it.
The new is unfamiliar. It may be a friend.
It may be an enemy. Who knows?
And there is no way to know.
The only way to know is to allow it.
Hence, the apprehension, the fear.

Osho

As humans, we are taught to avoid pain at all cost. Our entire life is set up by early brain conditioning to seek pleasure and avoid pain. Throughout my life, I have learned to lean-in a little more into pain and not to attempt to avoid it. I have actually found a way to savor pain just a little, to enjoy the excitement and potential danger of it without causing myself grievous harm or injury. I have, of course, suffered injuries of all sorts and pain across the spectrum. But by paying attention to the pain, I have come to see that it always has a message, every single time.

Pain is a warning, a reminder call from the body and mind that something is out of balance and may need my intervention to correct it. It can also be an indicator for me that some area of my development or life needs attention. I have studied pain in order to get better acquainted with it and to learn from it. One of the biggest aspects of this particular practice is information. Lack of awareness of the source of the pain, the increased fear of not knowing what harm it may be causing or might bring in the future seems to increase the intensity of pain.

I believe it is possible to shift our overall awareness—not only of our pain, but of our body and our life—by leaning in a little to our pain and by practicing being aware of, even welcoming, our pain as it appears. Any aspect of the four quadrants that you are not paying attention to may become neglected or under-developed. The net result of this will manifest in your life as difficulty, pain, shame, deficiency, or even loss.When I work with clients, I help them study, examine and ultimately embrace your pain as a teacher as part of your overall development plan. The body as a whole has far more wisdom in comparison to the relatively tiny brain's egotistical screeching and squawking and constant flow of information overload. Stepping into where you fear to live, bringing up the excitement around the edges of fear, keeps you in the constant awareness of your pain—even when you do not know the source or the outcome.

I am by no means suggesting to injure or punish yourself, but there may be an edge for each of you (it's always different) where the effort to stretch into or lean into small pains may lead to far larger gains.

I was working with a client who kept telling me about her pain and resistance. I consistently reframed it as her pain was stopping her from feeling some vital experiences. I pointed out the possibility that what she was fearing to explore around her pain might be fun! I used the phrase "Fun, Challenging and Exciting." These are the three edges upon which fear is built, and are usually hidden from conscious awareness—unless and until one is willing to do a little exploration. If you do not believe that what you fear may possibly be more "fun, challenging and exciting," you have already set yourself up for failure. The so called "traditional" notion of a pain-free life is both an illusion and a lie that we have been sold by quick-fix media. Nothing is guaranteed to be "easy." The nature of everything is to change. There is a constant flow from state to state, from form to form. Nothing is ever totally still for more than the merest moment.

If I truly believe that all I have to do is sit in meditation and visualize in order to bring waves of customers in the door without any conscious effort or attention to developing relationships, I may become very poor and wait an extremely long time. It is the acknowledgement and feeling the pain and fear and doing the next step anyway with awareness and vision that leads to the next level of growth.

The pain of fear of rejection is another frequently voiced concern and has an important effect on the outcome of your vision. If you are strong in living your vision as a place to come from and are listening deeply, then you are gifting yourself an enormous amount of energy right from the very start. Otherwise, it is the equivalent of having one foot pushed down on the gas pedal and the other equally held down of the brake. It will surely create a lot of energy, but it will be mostly inertia. You will be going nowhere fast. That is why the Monk pillar is so important, examining your beliefs.

It has been an important lesson for many of my clients stepping into their pain and fears and receiving what is called "disconfirming evidence." This is what develops when you step into your fear and pain and are pleasantly surprised to find love, encouragement and support for your efforts, rather than the expected rejection.

One of my clients who did public speaking for a living believed for a long time that he would die if he was rejected. It had even kept him from reaching out to people he already knew. He began to lean into that fear gradually—first with people he believed he could trust and then, eventually, in gently expanding increments to others he began to believe he could trust. As he did this, his self-awareness, confidence and business soared.

Some key questions to ask yourself: Does a rejection define you as a "loser" for all time? Is it a setback you can learn from? If you do not get the outcome you are seeking, does that mean you should just quit and try something else (perhaps to just fail there too)?

One aspect of my methodology is to deeply self-examine the areas where you are holding old energy or beliefs that stand in your way of accomplishing your vision. Examining these will help you shed light on the areas that may block your manifesting your vision.

The deep-seated pain in your life, your fear of rejection, of not being good enough, will certainly hinder your learning to move forward within your "not knowing." We live in "not knowing" but we want to think we have control and know. It feels safer to live in "knowing" but the reality is we really "don't know." This is a key element of your ongoing education about yourself. It can be very exciting to play in the "not knowing," and to lean into it. It can fire you up to see what you may discover about yourself in the process and be able to share that knowledge.

By always being open to try something new, to "not know" and do it anyway leads to continuous discovery of both self and others. Doing something different for yourself every day that is fun and healthy—joining a clean-up of a park or going for a walk, doing volunteer work, having a special day with your children, or your inner child. Be vulnerable and open to speak your truth. Make the phone call that is both scary and exciting. Sit in meditation longer than usual, or choose to sit in a different spot. These small challenges may open up new vistas in your awareness that let you examine those painful parts of your life that create fear and stop you from moving forward.

PART FOUR
CHAPTER THIRTY-ONE

Resistance

I often encounter resistance whenever I'm creating something new in my life in designing the future. I call that aspect of my work excitement and hopeful, expressing confidence in the future. The primary aspect of this experience is opening myself to embrace the new and fresh, to invite it in with joy and love. Resistance, no matter how much it might seem "proper," simply keeps the change from coming.

When I first worked within my group coaching, I did so with a long memory of my own learning challenges. I remembered extreme shame and the many difficulties I had with being bullied and the severe judgments of my teachers. I never once felt as if I were good enough, never felt I really belonged. At that time, my intention was to use the group to heal those old false beliefs and to establish my Legacy work. Part of my design was to support teachers and other visionaries with school projects for children with disabilities and other learning styles. Part of my intention was to interview teachers and review their teaching methods and learn how I could support their improvement in working with challenging students. Due to my old belief system as a dyslexic, I had serious resistance to talking to teachers.

My resistance was so strong that it initially stopped me from moving forward with my work. I found that I was completely blocking my own vital energy. I actually allowed an entire month to go by before I was able to feel the flow of energy through my body again.

In my group, I was given immediate support that allowed me to feel less isolated. It allowed me to eliminate my resistance and to speak openly about my fears of interviewing teachers. This opened me up to a greater feeling of confidence and opened me to a brand-new perspective and ease. Our working together to make a difference in education created a gigantic sense of connection and collaboration for all of us.

I have really immersed myself in my edge in creating live events and in writing this book. Both of these experiences are moving me forward on the track to the future I have envisioned and desired. By far the biggest has been to write this book. I hired my first book coach to go through this process with me. I hired two other very capable and experienced individuals who I have previously worked with to help create the live events. I am constantly having to meet my resistance and confront my old negative beliefs.

LIFE LESSONS

1. While it is challenging for you to be out of your comfort zone, it does not have to be threatening.

2. Challenge can be healthy and stimulating if you do not allow your fear, resistance or other emotions to hold you back from moving forward.

3. All fear is energy and potential excitement, fun and challenging.

4. Sharing your vision and excitement with others will inspire them to want to work with you.

5. Not feeling you have to do it all alone allows you to create in ways you never dreamt possible.

6. By sharing your fears and being open to them, you encourage others to open to their fear and resistance.

Celebrate Your "No"

I challenge my clients to go out and purposely fail and get a "No" or to really screw something up in public so that they can have the experience of not being "perfect." This experience helps them learn to not take it personally and to learn something new about themselves so they try new things and stretch into their vision.

What is the one thing that would really fire you up, that would challenge you tremendously? In what arena could you find the most difficult, yet achievable challenge and really be vulnerable? Where you could let your guard down and be told No?

Keep track of how many rejections or "No's" you get in the next week. You might get some "Yeses," but your object is to lean into the process and allow yourself to lessen the fear of taking a risk. You actually want to get the "No." This process will get you out of your head and move you into play mode. Track them all, watch where they come up in the context of your life. Be bold. Be courageous.

Celebrate your "No" every time you get one. Celebrate the fact that you took the chance, and may be getting closer to getting a "Yes." Acknowledge the "No" so that you can risk growing larger and more confident. Every "No" will teach you more about yourself and what steps you might take to improve your opportunities. Celebrate a "No."

PART FOUR
CHAPTER THIRTY-TWO

Openness

Open your heart. Open your mind.

Satyen Raja, Living Ecstasy

Openness for me means being available to possibility. Even more, paying attention to the energies and opportunities being presented allows my heart to be vulnerable and transparent. In a sense, it is what I call being "naked" all the time. When I speak my truth and allow myself to share my deepest and truest emotions, either with loved ones or in a public format, it increases my ability to be real and to be in my power.

I really look at this openness as a muscle. The more that I purposely allow myself to open my heart, the more present and loving I feel with all my relations and all circumstances around me. It doesn't happen overnight. I can close my openness off if I do not literally work "whole-heartedly" with conscious awareness.

Openness is the original state in which you were born. The longer you live, the more accumulated memories of experiences stick to you. One of the main purposes of all of this work is learning to be aware of the energies in your own body and those around you. Of course, it is always important to pay attention to the relative safety of each moment. Being open does not mean being foolish, careless or without boundaries. Openness fluctuates in response to circumstances. Being open to yourself and to those around you allows you to choose to take action where needed.

I had a very vivid experience of this one day when I was at the airport. I saw a woman with her three kids. She was urgently whispering to her five-year-old son telling him that he should go into the men's room in the busy airport by himself. He looked extremely uncomfortable. As I walked by, I was aware of his discomfort. I was tempted for a moment to ignore the energy and just walk away. But then I responded to what I saw as an opportunity to assist the mother with the little boy. I offered to accompany the child into the bathroom. Then, I followed him out and returned him to his mom. I really felt good for having paid close attention to his needs and the situation more than myself.

Listening is a key ingredient—listening with curiosity, childlike wonder and compassion, and being open to the moment and taking action when you are called.

I gave a very memorable talk once. I was fully vulnerable and transparent on stage, speaking my truth flat-out. I was laughing, sharing jokes and insights from my life. I even broke into tears and shared personal ideas and understandings that had touched me deeply. It completely rocked my world. I worked up to that level of intensity and honesty. I had been showing up that way regularly every day with my family and clients but never before a large audience.

Standing there, I was being completely "real" and honest, sharing my very deepest truths out of a genuine desire to share and connect with transparency. Bringing my passion and all of my feelings—joy, fear, shame, even anger—lit up the audience. It was impossible to ignore. Every person there was touched by who I really was without manipulation or coercion. My vulnerability, excitement and joy were an invitation. People spontaneously responded because I touched their hearts.

WRITING EXERCISE: Openness

Let's look at where you are open. Take a seat, get comfortable and close your eyes. Breathe deeply and comfortably until you feel settled in your center.

1.   Make a list of everything that has brought you joy and happiness in the past week.

2.   What three would you share with your closest circle of friends? Who would you share with and to what depth?

3.   What one would you choose purposely NOT to share with anyone? Why?

4.   Now do the same exercise making a list of the difficult or painful experiences of the week.

PART FOUR
CHAPTER THIRTY-THREE

Creating the Impossible

"There is no use in trying," said Alice. "One can't believe in impossible things."
"I dare to say, you haven't had much practice," said the Queen. "When I was your age, I always did it for a half hour a day. Why, sometimes I'd even believe as many as six impossible things before breakfast."

Impossible Dreams, Lewis Carroll,
"Alice in Wonderland."

Many times in my past I created the seemingly impossible in my own life—even though my brain chatter wanted to discount or discourage this.

You can focus on something being possible, or not. Every time I attempt to focus on something I do NOT want, it inevitably occurs. There's an old saying: "Worry is advertising for what you don't want." I may repeatedly tell myself to not drive through a pothole on my mountain bike. As longs as I stay focused on the pothole, I am almost certainly going to hit it. If I tell myself, even just once, to avoid the hole and then turn my attention to the safe path around it, I will stay focused on what is in front of me.

Almost everyone believes that maximum effort is required in attempting to attain your goals and desires, as if pushing harder is the solution. I have come to prefer the term "dancing" to make things happen. This implies finding an intimate flow that is somehow inherent in the process and the interaction that wants to happen. You can choose to make yourself available to open up to new possibilities, not to shut down and work even harder.

The very thought of creating the impossible can bring a sense of joy, exhilaration and passion in your body. I help clients find this sense in their body as they create their vision. It feels as if you are plugged into a massive magnetic source. You are in a tube that's vibrating intensely, drawing everything to it without any effort. It just seems to happen automatically, naturally. The only caveat is that, if you disconnect from that source, the energy immediately changes. My job is to help you own that rich, wonderful passion for creating your vision, holding it with you as your own passion builds and you learn to carry it with you everywhere.

One Mankind weekend retreat, my mentor was operating as Materials Coordinator. It was the very first training I had with him. He was filled with passion and electric energy, beaming joy and confidence. I so wanted to be his right-hand man. I felt like a puppy dog following him around. He was so lit up, so on-purpose, so magnetic, I could not help but want to follow his lead. I knew this was the energy I wanted to bring to my life. What I learned is that any time your energy starts lessening even if it is a challenging time, it is time to reassess your approach and relax. Is it a time to rest or is it a time of resistance and ego self-chatter?

Repetition and practice reinforce your vision and disrupt your resistance and ego chatter. The joyous and easy muscle needs to be worked regularly to stay in top shape—even with those you don't know or with those you feel might not return it. Ultimately the work is about you. You're using your own energy. This is the true reward. As I always remind myself: "This is my training ground! Bring it on! Next. Next. Next."

The more you practice working from your vision, the more love, time and effort you put into it, the more you practice, the more it becomes real and you manifest your vision in the world.

PART FOUR
CHAPTER THIRTY-FOUR

Play Bigger

A diamond is just a chunk of coal that is made good under pressure.

Henry Kissinger

We are All Diamonds

We are all born diamonds. Then, we begin to get tainted by the distractions and experiences of everyday life, including our childhood wounded stories. In The Dojo, you learn skills to remove the overlay of emotions, shame and pain that were added to cover your initial brilliance. I have always wanted to have it all removed at once, but I have reluctantly come to find that is not how life operates. It is an on-going life time process. In The Dojo we work together to carefully remove layer by layer so you can be more present for yourself, your family and your work.

In my work it was my intention to get that diamond shining

clear and brightly. Even when I thought I was playing full out, my coach called me on it, and he knew I was "brilliant" and could "play bigger."

In my own work that first year, I sat back and watched. I knew I was not bringing my full leadership potential to the table. I knew I was not owning myself or playing full-out. I knew I was holding back. The following year, I amped up to eighty percent. I genuinely believed that I wanted to be at one hundred percent, to be authentic, and to take all the risks and fears, and to reach my vision. I wanted to walk my talk and live it and to teach it. I wanted to really bring that power and energy into my work and relationships with everyone I came into contact. I wanted to be a leader across the board and stop shrinking.

Breaking through the shell surrounding my brilliance was a commitment to myself, to create something awesome and incredible for myself. Removing that shell required that I go through the process of experimenting, even when there was no guarantee of success or of gaining greater confidence.

I had a client break through his shell by making a commitment to be in my group for a year. He removed layers of mental and emotional "dirt". He continued moving forward even at times when he was unsure of where he was going or how he was going to get there. He had made a decision, a true commitment to experiment with who he was and where he wanted to go, to follow his vision.

I am still a diamond that is getting cleared of old and antiquated materials that have accumulated. I love deeply and am a person of service. Putting that aspect of myself up-front in all of my relationships elevates my ability to give and to shine in the process and helps my clients reach their true brilliance.

Empowerment Calendar

One of my goals is to work with you to create an "Empowerment Calendar" and to actually fill each day with everything that is important to you. You assign each event a time and space, making all of them equally important—appointment with a client, a massage or working out, meditations, or time with your wife and children. By doing this, you bring your best attention and effort to everything. This supports your work in all the four quadrants of your life simultaneously.

I work with you to create your calendar. You can even block out time off, time to do absolutely nothing. Blocking off time to do absolutely nothing was very trippy for me. "It's okay to sit down, just vegetate and chill"—giving it the same importance as all of my "tasks." When you do this, you can actually concentrate one hundred percent on each section of your day.

I call this type of scheduling my "Empowerment Calendar." It includes legacy/work, physical self-care, relationships and spiritual. It's a life-balancing calendar, bringing together your personal needs with your professional demands, and making them equally important. If I am not bringing together all four quadrants, I am not operating at my fullest potential. Focusing on all of the quadrants in my life improves my business exponentially because I have the energy and support to be present one hundred percent in all I do.

Three Sports a Day

As an elite athlete, training has always been part of my life. I operate at my very best when I train hard and have fun. Participating in three sports a day optimizes my energies. This has become my everyday benchmark. Three Sports a Day can include play, workout, sex, biking, walking, putting your feet in the sand, meditation, massage, dancing, singing. Any of them can be spiritual, physical, or relationship oriented.

When I was 19, I made a choice to open my first business. My business plan was, and still is, to work hard and to live as if I am already retired by doing what I love to do. I love meeting new people and creating deep relationships. At that time, I had no idea that my philosophy would take me to the next level of growth and awareness.

I was drawn to wake boarding from the very first. Within a year of opening my first business, I was wake boarding five days a week. By the following year, I had moved into a house on the water, was training for competition and had a boat in my backyard. Sometimes I would ride two to three times a day. By 6:30 AM, I would have meditated, done some yoga and taken a hot tub. By 7 AM I would be waiting for my training partners to show up. Usually, I would have a three-sport day before 8 AM.

After ten years of competing and training in a very driven manner without listening to my body, I was in a lot of pain. I made up that the answer was to stop training and work harder at my business. I hired a business coach, stopped all my training and focused on creating money. My business grew very fast and I wanted to look good for my coach. Like sports, it felt easy. I believed I could train hard in business without injuring or damaging my body, even though I was in constant pain.

I was living on ibuprofen, alcohol and marijuana, attempting to ignore my body and all my pain. I was only sleeping two hours a night, and had very effectively blocked out all of my emotions and bodily feelings. I'd been stuffing my creativity and every opportunity to play, stuffing my soul to be a better businessman. I truly believed that is what everyone wanted me to be, including myself. It seemed as if I was invisible to myself and others. I kept up my arduous schedule, working long hours away from my family, not paying attention to my body, not taking care of my relationships, or spiritual practice. Everyone else thought I was doing great, yet I was feeling more miserable and alone than ever in my life. I desperately needed something to change. There was a time when I had booked a massage. Before the appointment, I drank a few beers and smoked a bit of weed just to "calm down."

I thought that by ignoring my body and pushing hard for success, that I was on the track to becoming "successful." I was brutally wrong.

Eventually, I started training again with a new perspective. I made space in my life every day for my three sports. I was a broken elite athlete. I reached out for support to anchor-in this new way of being an athlete and a businessman. I had to learn to listen to my body and soul, and not give up. I began rehabilitating my body, my business practices and all my relationships back to health. I have found it to be priceless on my journey.

LIFE LESSONS

1.   Self-care is your number one task as an entrepreneur.

2.   Schedule three sports daily that frighten or exhilarate you to motivate yourself. You are worth it.

3.   Never give up. Always show up and listen to your body.

PART FOUR
CHAPTER THIRTY-FIVE

Practice, Practice, Practice

You should be grateful for the weeds you have inyour mind, because eventually they will enrich your practice.

Suzuki Roshi

There will always be plateaus in your life where further progress seems impossible. This can be very frustrating. If you continue to practice, you will inevitably improve. Mastery lies in recognizing that a plateau is an improvement from the previous plateau. In order to become a master, one must simply practice for the sake of practicing. Part of mastery is about loving the plateau. Part of the mastery is taking time to allow the plateau to inform you.

Practicing taking action even when you are not feeling like it will strengthen your ability to not be influenced by your temporary emotional state. I like to say that, "Feeling good is not a requirement. It is a result." This is a practice.

I give myself credit for making the time to care for myself. This is a necessary part of my practice. My practice is to create the space necessary so that I have the inner resources to give one hundred percent. Now, I schedule a week off from work for the final week of the month. I call it our integration week. I have found that by doing this self-care that I am more productive, creative and my business grows. All quadrants in my life are enhanced. I tend to really like Fridays. My schedule says meditation, Cross-Fit, and immediately below that, "Off." I'm not allowed to put anything else in there. Amber has busted me so many times for it. "You've got a phone call right there. What's that? That's not off." I may argue a little, and I value for her input.

It sometimes feels uncomfortable as mind my says, "Work, work". This is a practice for me. But I know that the time I schedule for work is very important, and my time off and for self-care is just as important.

I deserve taking the time to practice. Everything I do has an impact on my family, my clients and everyone I contact. I practice because I'm worth it. When I practice, I am actually better in every area of my life. Practice. Practice. Practice.

Attached to Outcomes and Beliefs

When we work in the Dojo your vision is not your destination. It is where you come from. From this place of vision, you are open to listening to the Samurai for your next step and are open to change directions if that is what is called for.s Usually, the outcomes become far better than you could ever imagine or dream of. It doesn't look like you thought; but you feel integrated, whole and happier in all areas of your life.

When you are attached to an outcome, you will not be able to shift and be transformed. Such a rigid position can easily prevent you from moving forward in your life and leave you unable to be open to seeing anything in any other way.

Often unchanging attitudes and beliefs are rooted deeply in your past. The past beliefs can cause you to hold on tightly to what is often called "tradition," in order to not change or to not accept change even if what you are doing doesn't fit your life now and doesn't reflect where you want to be.

Attachment to old beliefs and attitudes can definitely keep you from speaking your truth and acting on it. When the deep energy of unspoken truth lives in your body and is not expressed properly, the accumulated weight does not just go away and is not forgotten. It gathers, concretizes, condenses and becomes even more difficult to express. Your truth must be expressed or it will ultimately cause some kind of disturbance.

The more easily and readily you are able to respond ("responsibility") to what your body feels and are able to speak it, the less accumulation there will be; and there will be less of a gap in your own consciousness between inside and outside. The most difficult times in my life have come when I, for whatever "good" reason, shut down and failed to express my bold truth. In The Dojo you learn to express these stuck attitudes and to speak your truth even just to yourself following your vision. Most of us start to be conditioned ("brainwashed") as children into believing that to express the truth is offensive, harmful, selfish, or "pushy." This kind of belief is frequently projected onto children by adults who cannot be honest with themselves or others. Children are often expected to defer to adults even when they may have the clearest, brightest, and most unencumbered view. As we age, we become increasingly divorced from truth, especially raw human emotional truth. The older we get, the more we are caught up in ridiculous social conventions and blind obedience to a non-feeling system that punishes us for being real.

In The Dojo you will become brutally honest with yourself and you will accomplish more—more training, more work, more enjoyment, more fulfillment and more success. What others might condemn as "pushy" can actually be healthy self-care. I experience my most powerful self when I feel strong, bold and loving, filled with the possibility, and unafraid to express my most vulnerable thoughts, needs and deeds freely.

Everyone has "bad days." They are an inescapable part of the human condition. As someone once said, "Pain is to be expected, suffering is optional." In the Dojo you constantly work on understanding yourself and knowing you are doing the best you can with the knowledge you have. The more clearly and cleanly you work on the relationship you have with yourself, the more you can optimize your fulfillment in all areas of your life. You can choose, on a daily basis, to show up how you want to be—not at the mercy of shifting moods, fixed outcomes or a temporary bad attitude (no matter the reason). You can choose to bring your full truth into the light so that you can motivate yourself and others by being a living example of your own transformation.

Most of us are our own Number One Critic. We beat ourselves up more than anyone else we know. Within The Dojo you learn that when this happens, it is important to remember not to get stuck in the old wounded stories and become attached to certain outcomes. Reminding yourself of your vision and being grateful for the little things in your life, you create a deeper attitude of gratitude. This attitude of gratitude is then reflected everywhere in your life, constantly mirroring in your relationship with others and moving you forward to creating your visions.

Through loving yourself, you create your own lived reality. If the world that you want to create is a world of love, then it's really only by vigilantly loving yourself that you may accomplish it. If the world you want to create is as a balanced Integrated Leader, then live from that vision. The more you activate and play with the energy of Creation, the more you manifest from that place.

The Dojo is the training ground for developing the next level of connection you want in your life. Consistently bringing the same kind of energy across the board in all of your life activities in all quadrants is how you create the world you want to live in. Even though you may not be able to always show up one hundred percent, in The Dojo you will constantly be improving every area of your life. You will feel more fulfilled and successful.

Sometimes when you have made a big achievement, or let go of old wounded stories and attitudes and try something new, you may want to withdraw or even hibernate (I call it "communing with my little boy.") There is a normal ebb and flow to everyone's energy. After having an intense experience, it may be difficult to return home to everyday life. It's totally acceptable to be in the ebb state, knowing it will not be permanent. It's necessary and proper to honor the need to move inward and flow with it.

UJI (oo-gee): Flow

I was recently talking to my son Bodhi about Uji. Roshi Andrew Shugyo Daijo Bonnici, Ph.D., defines Uji as a still timeless intelligent moment that is always happening everywhere, all at once, throughout the whole universe while being felt as a precious stillness arising from our body's center-point of gravity.

Ugi means Being Timeless Time in Japanese. How can I be in structured time but also experience below that to a space of timelessness? How do I live in the Ugi, or Now time, with schedules and structure? Some people experience Ugi when they are meditating, praying, in nature, or physical activities. It is the space below everyday life that you can touch and experience that allows you to be guided beneath the structures imposed by your thoughts or society. It is a space that allows you to move beyond your self-imposed limitations.

Zen practice is very formal and very structured. For years, I fought the structure. Through the many years of resistance, of trial and error, I finally came to see that on my 3 x 3 meditation mat I found freedom as I followed my breath and let go of my "monkey mind". I came to realize that I could use the structure to accommodate and accentuate my needs and choices. I could use the structure to enhance and uplift my freedom in being me. It allowed me to move beyond my "thinking mind" limitations.

It can really be a struggle to live within the expectations and structures of our everyday life. Yet you can experience freedom. I have this space that says, "How can I express me in the practice of my life? How can I live my truth when I'm working on the book? How can I be me at work or with my children?" I realize that I can experience structure as fluid and not rigid or solid. Many of my structures are self-imposed. I can make choices that allow my true expression in my work/legacy, physical, relationships, and spiritual life. Now some structures in society are needed and necessary, but I can navigate them easier if I come from a place of "flow" and listening to my truth.

Living my life practicing Ugi, or being in the "flow" and living this moment, I feel guided to make the best choice. It is in this structure of letting go that I can listen to my truth and live it.

WRITING EXERCISE: Ugi

Where do you experience Ugi?

AN
INVITATION

Part Five

PART FIVE
CHAPTER THIRTY-SIX

Transformation

When you think you're at your full potential, you are really only operating at forty percent of your capability.

Jesse Itzler

Renée

Renée and I have become friends and continue to work closely together. We have weekly sessions where we collaborate to broaden her dreams, and continuously challenge her to upgrade her belief system. She is constantly seeking to actualize the life she has always wanted of being of pure service and making an impact on the planet. Her movement center is the largest in Honolulu. She has taken The Still and Moving Center on-line and global. Currently the curriculum and methods are taught in five languages in seven different countries. She is extremely humble yet absolutely beautiful and powerful. She daily lives her mission of seeing and bringing out the magnificence in everyone she meets, especially her employees.

As a dynamic leader, she has found that her natural vitality grows the more she gives. Deepening her relationship with her children and grandchildren has proven to be a foundational catalyst for the continuing development of her business and her legacy-work.

John

After our first year of working together, John made the decision to dissolve the company he had run for the previous fifteen years in order to begin again, to create the new world he had envisioned, and to live the authentic person he is now. He now trusts that his new way of living as an Integrated Leader is firmly rooted in abundance and value.

John has become deeply trusting of his daily spiritual practice as a way of connecting to his truth and core. He's fully involved in his health and self-care. He challenges himself daily in many creative ways. John is connecting deeper with his partner, being open and vulnerable as he has never been before. He is leading the company he has always dreamed of. His daily life is a continual process that involves his being constantly on his mission and making a difference in the world as an Integrated Leader.

Jason

Jason ran his first half-marathon within six months of our working together. He declares that he is "still carrying the energy of it into his company." Jason later remarked that the whole process for him was about dealing with "discomfort, pain and fear." When he finished that run, he said he was "so exhilarated that he had done something his mind said he could never do." He said he had "never felt so alive." As a result of our work, Jason now views being a father to his four boys as his top priority. He now sees his work with relationships with women as a continuation of his work on himself, relating from a place of authenticity and honesty.

Jason always understood that the vision was not a place get to, but a place to come from on a daily basis in all areas of his life. His company is doing better than ever. He is using his new awareness and sharing this desire at work to create a more vibrant, integrated and healthier environment.

He now mentors and runs multiple men's groups as part of his stated legacy work of bringing families together. He has found his own voice around his mission and is using it to make an impact on others around the world. He has become a model of integrity in all four quadrants. He is living as an Integrated Leader, a position that he is constantly refining.

Bruce

Bruce continues to manifest his vision of changing the way fast-food restaurants operate. He is making an impact in the world by serving only high-quality, plant-based foods. He embodies and promotes a high standard of respect and interaction with all of his employees which translates into quality customer service. He now has stores on both the North and South Islands of New Zealand, and still has designs to expand into other countries with partners who share his vision as well as his love and compassion for humanity and desire to make a difference on the planet. Bruce continues to strengthen his relationship with his wife and children. He is committed to his own health, self-care and well-being. He continues to listen to his inner guidance.

PART FIVE
CHAPTER THIRTY-SEVEN

Join Me in The Dojo

I have created my life so that I can live as an Integrated Leader. My spiritual practice guides me to listen deeply to my next step. I get up at 4 AM each morning to cuddle with Amber, meditate, do yoga, vision and write. My relationship with Amber is amazing as we encourage each other to grow as individuals and as a couple. We have weekly dates and daily check-ins. We are a major part of each other's business. We share ideas and encourage each other to dream the impossible and create it. I have powerful relationships with my boys, Sage and Bodhi. I take them at 5:30 AM to the beach to spear fish or body surf. We go every afternoon to the gym together. I am ready to start working at 8 AM.

My business has grown in ways I could have never imagined. I am changing lives and seeing my clients live their dreams. I am seeing them experience more fulfilling and happier lives. I only work with a total of five deeply dedicate entrepreneurs every calendar year. I do one-on-one coaching, weekend intensives, and VIP Days. I feel grateful to be able to journey with my clients—changing lives, holding visions, encouraging people to live beyond what they could ever have dreamed.

This book is about transformation. It is about changing your life to be an Integrated Leader by sharing my journey and methodology to change your life. This is transformation in all areas of your life—work/legacy, physical, relationships and spiritual. It is about learning to live as an Integrated Leader, challenging yourself in every area of your life. One area affects all the areas. You will find unimagined success in your business, greater connection in all your relationships, you will create time for self-care and connection to your inner knowing.

This journey is about meeting in the Dojo, a place of brutal honesty with yourself. In the Monk pillar you examine old wounds and core beliefs that stop you from living your highest potential. In the Sage pillar, you create visions that will bring your highest potential in all areas of your life, dreaming bigger than you could ever even imagine. You learn to live from this vision—not as a destination but as place to come from and live Now.

In the Samurai pillar you listen deeply to the next action steps you need to take to make your experience of your Vision come true. You live the felt experience and attitude of this vision being true Now by being guided so that your work/legacy, physical, relationship, and spiritual quadrants of your life feel fulfilled and successful.

In the Sensei pillar you live as an Integrated Leader. You bring all four quadrants together and share with the people around you in your work and in your personal life so that they feel supported to succeed and become their highest potential. You will work on the legacy you want leave behind for your family, your work and the world. How do you want to be remembered?

This is not easy work. It takes dedication, drive and a willingness to open up to new areas of success, challenge, and fulfillment in your life. Would you like to have a successful, meaningful business? Would you like to be able to take care of your self-care and your physical body? Would you like to have a better relationship with your family or with your partner? Would you like to connect with your inner knowing?

If you want to step into The Dojo and become an Integrated Leader, my Coaching is for you. Together we will manifest what you want in your life in the most fulfilling and successful way possible. To dream your impossible dream and to live it, come join me in The Dojo.

Find out more information at www.tonybonnici.com

I'm grateful to Tony and I recommend him highly as Business Coach. Tony Bonnici has been an invaluable help to me. Our experience working together not only boosted my confidence, but has given me a new view of who I am as a person. Tony's business coaching has given me a perspective on my legacy. He has encouraged me not only to focus growing my business and legacy, but to not lose sight of my relationships, spiritual practice and self-care. Attendance in my classes is up 150%. My outlook and attitude for the future is up 1000%. Working with Tony has made a real difference in how I value myself.

- Renée Tillotson, Founder of The Still & Moving Center and The Mindful Movement Academy

I hold the utmost respect for Tony, and the care and support he provided for me during the course of our work together.

He was masterful at holding space for me to challenge myself and achieve my goals. He always held a vision of me continually evolving into my best self. He created all of this while listening intently and showing what it means to be an Integrated Leader. He was always focused, authentic, vulnerable and loving in his coaching and consulting.

- Brad Bowers, CEO of BlackInc

When I started working with Tony, I was very present to and up against my own glass ceiling. I was aware that I wanted to break through it to the next level for a few years. So, we started our journey of uncovering my patterns, and deep ways of operating, that had been keeping me stuck for decades.

First, Tony taught me how to meditate properly and then signed me up for a half marathon to get moving. Holy Shit! I hadn't run for over 20 years and had exactly 6 months to train for a twenty-one-kilometer run! I did five and a half months of weekly physical therapy, and this changed my life and showed me what I could actually do.

I learned that the pain and resistance was mental. What I thought my body could handle and what it could actually do were miles apart. Now I'm a runner!

This kind of discipline and concentration paid dividends in all the other areas of my life as well. Tony coached me in a way that supported my own healing. He inspired me to look at everything, leaving no stone unturned.

It is through his coaching that I started the journey to becoming myself when I interacted with everyone. I used to struggle with speaking to managers and CEOs who I always judged to be more powerful than myself. Tony helped me to develop and own my innate power and equality.

I`m happy to report I have not felt my glass ceiling since. I`m more confident, open and in charge of all the areas of my life. Tony`s work is powerful, subtle, integral and changed me from within. I`m forever grateful for the time we spent together and count Tony as a personal friend.

- Jason Seaward,
CEO and Founder of Motion Recruitment

Tony helped me keep my eyes fixed on my bigger picture and vision: the fundamental 'why' of my chucking my architectural career and stepping into a plant-based fast-food business. I believe we exist to disrupt the incumbents in our industry, to make a positive difference for the environment for both animals and humans, and by helping people transition to plant-based eating.

Tony's coaching was especially crucial in my regaining my self-belief, especially when I was buckling under the weight of the many demands (general and sometimes-debilitating) ups and downs of just being in business.

I'm happy to say that Tony's coaching has continued to be a factor in my company's continuing success and growth. Keeping the negative mind talk in its rightful place (i.e., consigned to the trash!) allows me to stay completely focused the big picture and my vision.

- Bruce Craig, CEO of Lord of the Fries

Tony Bonnici is a superb business coach. I worked with Tony in 2011-'12. I was seeking a greater connection in my relationships with myself and others as well a deeper link to both my life purpose and businesses. Tony and I designed learning experiences that immersed me in the totality of Nature, including intensive coaching sessions, meditation, journaling, yoga, and extended time for self-care. I experienced myself in a totally new way, re-embodying my skills as an Integrated Leader. Tony's support was invaluable to me.

- Michael Bonahan,
CEO of Wisdom Windfall, Former Director of Boys to Men, Hawaii

As an executive coach, author, and consultant, I am very discerning on what makes an effective coach. Over my career, I have engaged more than 7 coaches. While they all were effective in one area or another, Tony is the first coach that really listened to me and believed in my dreams. He has helped me to achieve my life goals and kept me on track to reach a higher potential with joy. How I achieved results and the person I have become over the last six months is motivating me to continue on the path. I lost 35 pounds, improved my outlook, attracted a strong team of project managers, researchers, consultants, educators, and writers, increased revenues, wrote 10,000 words on a new book, and have a new strategic direction for my company which is working. Simply an amazing fun experience in a short time of six months of focused coaching and performance. I highly recommend if you get an opportunity to work with Tony, you say "Yes."

- Jackie Lyles- Bestselling Author,
Founder of Business Champion Sales Method

Tony helped me to transform my life. Several years ago, I was unhappy with my job and was searching for a spiritual identity. Tony helped me to find my answers from within. I made the switch to a career that I am truly passionate about, and also have a strong spiritual connection. Thanks, Tony!

- Steve Caria, CEO at Jedi Management

Tony is one of the most powerful, deep, wise empowering passionate, grounded spiritual men I have met in my life.

- Reverend Kelly Childress,
Founder of Crossroads Coaching & Consulting

Tony is one of the most passionate men I've ever met about personal transformation both in the terms of entrepreneurship and leadership. He unlocked something powerful within myself, my business, and my relationships.

- James Butler, Founder, and CEO of Reclaiming Warrior

I would suggest anyone come and experience Tony, as an opportunity to look at those things keeping you from being who you want to be, keeping you from your highest potential.

- Tony Barett, Owner of The AJB Company

Our challenge before was really our business identity, who we were in the marketplace, our values, the contribution we deliver to our clients. We needed to grow. Just 8 weeks in, we had an increased sales volume, brewing volume, and new clients coming on board. Our new sense of identity has completely changed how I am being in the business and the growing vision for where we are going. If first and foremost you want a balance between your professional life and your personal life, I`d encourage you to get in touch with Tony.

- René Archner, Founder and Chief Brewer at René`s Kombucha